Conservation Heroes

THEODORE ROOSEVELT

Conservation Heroes

Conservation Heroes

THEODORE
ROOSEVELT

Brad Fitzpatrick

CHELSEA HOUSE
An Infobase Learning Company

Theodore Roosevelt

Copyright ©2011 by Infobase Learning

Chelsea House
An imprint of Infobase Learning
132 West 31st Street
New York, NY 10001

Library of Congress Cataloging-in-Publication Data
Fitzpatrick, Brad.
    Theodore Roosevelt / Brad Fitzpatrick.
        p. cm. — (Conservation heroes)
    Includes bibliographical references and index.
    ISBN 978-1-60413-948-8
    1. Roosevelt, Theodore, 1858-1919—Juvenile literature. 2. Presidents—
United States—Biography—Juvenile literature. 3. Conservationists—United
States—Biography—Juvenile literature. 4. Nature conservation—United
States—History—Juvenile literature. I. Title. II. Series.
    E757.F47 2010
    973.91'1092—dc22
    [B]   2010026475

Chelsea House books are available at special discounts when purchased in
bulk quantities for businesses, associations, institutions, or sales promotions.
Please call our Special Sales Department in New York at (212) 967-8800 or
(800) 322-8755.

You can find Chelsea House on the World Wide Web at
http://www.chelseahouse.com.

Text design and composition by Annie O'Donnell
Cover design by Takeshi Takahashi
Cover printed by Bang Printing, Brainerd, MN
Book printed and bound by Bang Printing, Brainerd, MN
Date printed: January 2011
Printed in the United States of America

10 9 8 7 6 5 4 3 2 1

This book is printed on acid-free paper.

Contents

A Dangerous Hunt

Theodore Roosevelt, the twenty-sixth president of the United States, left office in 1908. "Teddy," as the American public called him, was a man who had always loved being outdoors. Thus, after he left office, he set out for Africa on an expedition to collect animals for the Smithsonian Museum in Washington, D.C. Roosevelt's son Kermit accompanied his father on his African adventure. Together, they hunted several species of game and sent the skins and skulls of the animals back to the United States so that scientists could examine these species. Many of the skins the Roosevelts sent back to the United States were from animals that the Smithsonian scientists had only seen in illustrations in books.

Roosevelt and Kermit hunted in the British colonies of Uganda, Sudan, and Kenya. They rode on horseback, accompanied by a huge crew that helped them carry supplies, set up tents, track and skin game, clear brush, and cook. The safari crew numbered more than 200 individuals and sometimes stretched out over half a mile as they followed the Roosevelts.

Theodore Roosevelt (*center left,* with his son, Kermit) went hunting in East Africa in 1910, along with a huge safari crew.

HUNTER AND CONSERVATIONIST

Theodore Roosevelt loved being in the wilderness and had spent
much of his life collecting and examining specimens of wild animals. During his time as president, he had worked extremely hard
to protect wildlife and their habitats so that future generations of
Americans could also enjoy them. It had also been a dream of Roosevelt's since he was a boy to travel to Africa and see its animals.
Even though Roosevelt was hunting animals to send back to the
Smithsonian, he was also helping to protect those species he hunted
by supplying scientists in the United States with skins and skulls, as
well as written accounts of the numbers and behaviors of species he
had seen. The scientists, in turn, would study Roosevelt's specimens
and his journals to learn more about these animals.

The Roosevelts slept in tents during their journey. Often, these heavy, green canvas tents would be pitched near water or a native village. Roosevelt spent the mornings and evenings hunting (the times when the animals he was looking for were most likely to be on the move) and spent the early afternoon and nighttime hours writing about his adventures and reading books.

Roosevelt had often tested himself in the wildest places. He had been a rancher on the plains of North Dakota, hunted bears in the swamps of Louisiana and Mississippi, and led troops in battle in the tropical rainforests of Cuba. His father had taught him the value of outdoor activities such as running, horseback riding, tennis, hunting, and fishing. Growing up, Roosevelt learned to love the outdoors and spent much of his life in the wilderness. He believed that a healthy life was a balance of education and "vigorous outdoor activity." In his autobiography, Roosevelt explained, "Love of outdoor life, love of simple and hardy pastimes, can be gratified by men and women who do not possess large means, and who work hard. . . ."

Yet nothing that Roosevelt had done in the past could truly prepare him for hunting lions in Africa. In fact, more than anything else, Roosevelt wanted to hunt a lion. Since he was a boy, he had read about lions and lion hunters and wanted to see these powerful animals in the wild. He also wanted to test his bravery as he faced the big cat, an animal that can weigh more than 400 pounds (181 kilograms). Lions were considered one of the "Big 5" of African animals, along with the leopard, Cape buffalo, elephant, and rhinoceros. Still, it was the lion that Roosevelt wanted to hunt the most.

Roosevelt's party was camped in an area called Sotik in the East African country of Kenya, its string of green tents pitched near a small lake, or waterhole, as it is called in Africa. Several small, rocky hills surrounded the camp, and game animals grazed on the short, yellow grass of the plain and browsed on the leaves of the flat-topped acacia trees. At night, Roosevelt read, wrote, and listened to the calls of hyenas and baboons or to the faraway roaring of lions hunting in the night. During the day, Roosevelt and Kermit were led by their hunting guides out into the savanna in search of animals.

ROOSEVELT GETS HIS LION

One day, the group stopped at a waterhole to let their horses have a drink. Roosevelt noticed that Kermit's horse had hurt its leg and could not go any further. Kermit wanted to continue on with the hunting party, so he followed along on foot while his father and their safari guide, Leslie Tarleton, rode on across the plains

Because he was nearsighted, Theodore Roosevelt's glasses were helpful to him as he hunted.

CONSERVATION TODAY: THE SELOUS GAME RESERVE

During Theodore Roosevelt's lifetime, very little concern was given to protecting Africa's wildlife. Yet Roosevelt—along with many other conservationists and scientists—has since taught us how important it is to protect wild animals. Today, one of the world's largest game reserves, the Selous (*Su-LOO*) Game Reserve, is located not far from where Theodore Roosevelt hunted in Africa. Named after British explorer, hunter, and author Frederic Courtney Selous, the Selous Game Reserve was established in 1905 as a hunting park and later became a game reserve. The Selous is extremely large, covering almost 20,000 square miles (52,000 square kilometers) or 5 percent of the entire nation of Tanzania. Many rare species of birds and animals live in the Selous, including hippopotamuses, elephants, lions, leopards, and African wild dogs. Each year thousands of people visit the Selous, but there are no roads into the area and the most common way to reach the Selous is to fly into the Tanzanian city of Dar es Salaam and then take a small plane into the wilderness. In 1982, the Selous was named a World Heritage Site because of its importance to the preservation of African wildlife.

on their horses. Meanwhile, two of Roosevelt's trackers led Kermit's injured horse back to camp. Roosevelt, Kermit, and Tarleton stopped beside a *kopje* (pronounced *KOP-ee*), a small rocky hill, and looked for game across the grassy plain. Soon, they heard excited voices behind them and turned to see the trackers and the horse returning. The trackers told Roosevelt that they had come upon a very large male lion while they were leading the horse back to camp. Roosevelt mounted his horse, Tranquility, and galloped in the direction of the lion. Tarleton rode behind him. Kermit, who was without his horse, ran behind so that he would not miss out on the hunt.

They came upon the lion that had killed a zebra and was eating it on the open savanna. When the men approached on horseback, the lion stood, turned, and started trotting toward a large thicket. Roosevelt stepped down, took aim, and fired. His shot just grazed the lion's paw. The big cat started across the plains at a run, roaring and grunting as it went. Roosevelt fired again, this time shooting far behind the running cat.

For a hunter, very few things in the world are more dangerous than a wounded lion. But despite the danger, Roosevelt climbed back into the saddle and rode off after the cat. Leslie Tarleton followed behind, doing his best to see to it that the former President did not get hurt. Kermit knew that he would not be able to keep up with the men and so he climbed up on a nearby kopje to watch as his father and Leslie rode after the lion.

It was not long before the lion stopped and turned to face the men who were following it. It crouched in the long grass at the edge of the plains, growling and swinging its tail from side to side, a sign that it was about to charge. Yet Roosevelt showed no fear. He slid down off his horse and knelt on one knee, carefully aiming his rifle. Tarleton stepped down from his horse too and pulled his own rifle from its case. The lion grunted once more and then charged.

Roosevelt had lost the use of his left eye in a boxing match while he was president and so had to take very careful aim before firing. What's more, the lion was coming at him at 40 miles (65 km) per hour, covering 25 feet (8 meters) with every jump. If he missed, the lion would be upon him in 15 seconds and there would be very little that Tarleton could do to save him. Roosevelt knew all of these things, but if he felt afraid, he never let it show. He simply held the rifle steady and took careful aim.

When the lion was halfway to Roosevelt, roaring and grunting as it charged, Tarleton fired and missed, his bullet throwing a spray of dirt into the air behind the charging lion. Roosevelt pulled the trigger of his rifle. As the loud crack of the bullet echoed across the plains, the lion fell down in the dust. Roosevelt had stopped the charging cat and had saved his and Tarleton's lives.

TAXIDERMY

Theodore Roosevelt sent many of the animals that he shot in Africa back to the United States to be put on display in museums. Many of them were mounted for display by taxidermists. Taxidermists create lifelike replications of wild animals by stretching the animals' skins over foam forms. These skins must be very carefully handled to be sure that they will remain intact during shipping. Salt is applied to keep insects from ruining them. Glass eyes and plastic teeth give the final mount a very realistic look. Yet taxidermists do more than just mount animals. Many of them also raise colonies of special beetles called *dermestids* whose job is to remove meat and skin from an animal's bones so that its skeleton can be examined.

Taxidermy plays an important role in the study of animals. Several species that are now extinct can still be studied thanks to taxidermists. Many museums take dead animals and have them mounted so that in the future scientists and artists can examine the features of the animal. One of the most famous taxidermy mounts ever is that of Martha, the last passenger pigeon. After Martha died at the Cincinnati Zoo in 1914, she was mounted by taxidermists and visitors can now see what a passenger pigeon looked like, even though the real thing no longer exists.

There was much celebration when the safari crew arrived and began preparing the lion's skin to ship back to the scientists at the Smithsonian Institute in the United States. Kermit, meanwhile, had watched the entire chase and charge from the top of a rock.

It may be hard to imagine, but Theodore Roosevelt's hunting trip to Africa actually helped scientists to better understand the animals that Roosevelt sent home. At that time, very little was known about many of the animals that Roosevelt shot and wrote about. The skins, horns, and skeletons that Roosevelt sent back to America were a great source of data concerning African animals. Yet Roosevelt's trip to Africa accomplished something else. The rare and exotic animals that Roosevelt sent home to the United States caught the attention of the American public. His safari also began to help people around the world understand that wildlife had to be protected and studied.

Theodore Roosevelt accomplished many things while he was President of the United States. He made laws that required safe working conditions, helped to stop companies from employing children in dangerous jobs, and ensured that food sold in stores was safe to eat. But Theodore Roosevelt also protected something that was very valuable, something that was beginning to disappear from America in the early 1900s—he protected America's wildlife and, to help accomplish this, he also established its national parks. By protecting wild animals and their habitats, Roosevelt ensured that Americans for generations to come could enjoy the outdoors just as he had.

"Teedie," the Young Scientist

Theodore Roosevelt Jr. was born on October 27, 1858, at his family's home at 28 East 20th Street in New York City. His parents, Theodore and Martha Roosevelt, were well known in New York and often attended galas and balls with some of the city's wealthiest families. Theodore had a sister named Anna, who was three years older than he was. Most everyone in Theodore's family had a nickname and Anna's was "Bamie." Theodore was given the nickname "Teedie" by his father when he was a small child.

Despite being a wealthy family, the Roosevelts were very concerned with other people's welfare. Theodore's father spent a great deal of time and money helping those less fortunate. He organized the first Young Men's Christian Association (better known today as the YMCA) in New York City and donated his time and money to missionaries and boarding schools. The first meeting of the American Museum of Natural History was held in the front room of the Roosevelts' New York home. Yet Theodore's father did more than assist his fellow humans. He cared for animals too and was seen

The birthplace of Theodore Roosevelt, located at 28 East 20th Street in New York City, is seen here in 1923. Today, the Victorian town house is set up as a museum honoring Roosevelt.

driving his buggy down New York's crowded streets with kittens he had rescued riding in his front pocket.

Theodore Roosevelt Sr. was a tall, strong, athletic man. However, his son Theodore was a small, sickly child. Theodore Roosevelt Jr. was very young when doctors told his mother that he suffered from asthma, a condition that causes the tubes that lead into the lungs to swell. This, in turn, makes breathing difficult. Despite the doctor's best efforts, young Theodore suffered asthma attacks regularly. Oftentimes, he would have to sit up in bed for hours at night. On several occasions, he struggled so hard to breathe that his family did not know if he would survive until the morning.

The treatment people used for asthma at the time was black coffee, which Theodore was forced to drink regularly. The president would later say that the only thing that made him feel better was when his father held him in his arms. Neighbors oftentimes saw the Roosevelts' carriage racing along the streets at night with Theodore's father driving the horses as fast as they would go while he held his son in his arms in the hopes that cold night air would help stop an asthma attack. To make matters worse, Theodore suffered from diarrhea and a recurring nightmare that a werewolf was sneaking up to attack him in the night.

Young Theodore admired his father greatly and said he was "the best man I ever knew." So, when his father told him about the benefits of a rigorous outdoor life, Theodore paid careful attention. Despite his frequent asthma attacks, he enjoyed playing outside, especially in the woods. He climbed trees, rode horses, and liked to row a boat. Still, wild animals excited the young man most of all. Before Theodore could read, he carried books about natural history around with him and asked the older members of his family to read him the stories about the fascinating animals he saw in the book's images. Among young Theodore's favorite books was David Livingstone's *Missionary Travels and Researches in Southern Africa.* This book told of Livingstone's adventures in the largely unexplored southern portion of the African continent where unknown tribes and strange animals roamed. Another of Theodore's favorite authors was Charles Darwin, an Englishman who had traveled the world and described the different species he saw while on his trip. Theodore was especially interested in the comparisons that Darwin made between different species of birds and his thoughts on evolution. Roosevelt was also fascinated by Darwin's belief in natural selection and genetics.

THEODORE BECOMES A NATURALIST

One day, Theodore's mother sent him to the local market to buy fruit. Along the way, Theodore passed by the harbor where boats were unloading the day's catch of fish. One of the boats had brought in a dead seal and laid it out on the docks for everyone to see. Theodore was amazed. He had never touched a seal before, and now here was one that he could examine up close. He noticed how smooth the seal's fur was when it was wet, its long black whiskers, and the small toenails at the end of its flippers.

"The seal filled me with every possible feeling of romance and adventure," Theodore later said. He had found a unique scientific specimen to study for himself and felt just like his hero, Charles Darwin. Theodore returned to the harbor several more times to take measurements and record data about the seal in his journal. Roosevelt's instruments were crude—he later wrote that he did not have a tape to measure the girth of the seal and had to use a folding twelve-inch ruler. Just like Darwin, Theodore carefully recorded scientific data about the dead seal. Roosevelt kept all of his measurements in a notebook and wrote a simple story about the seal's life. Later, when the seal at the harbor was taken away and disposed of, Theodore was given the animal's skull.

The skull of a dead seal may not seem like a very exciting gift to most children. Theodore Roosevelt, however, could not have been more excited. The seal skull became the first specimen in Theodore's collection, which his family called "The Roosevelt Museum of Natu-

CHARLES DARWIN AND NATURAL SELECTION

Charles Darwin (1809–1882) was a British naturalist who developed a theory of evolution that is still embraced by most scientists around the world. Darwin made a voyage on a military ship called the HMS *Beagle*. During this journey, Darwin took careful note of the plants, animals, and fossils he collected along the way. One of Darwin's most famous observations involved finches living on the Galapagos Islands, located off the coast of Ecuador in South America. Darwin noticed that the finches all looked very similar except for their beaks. Some of the finches had small, thin beaks that were suitable for eating insects, while other finches had heavier beaks that were suitable for crushing fruit pits and seeds. This led Darwin to theorize that the finches had all started out as one single species and had evolved, or changed, over time to become separate species.

From here, Darwin developed the theory of natural selection. Natural selection states that organisms best suited for an environment will survive and reproduce while others will die off. As environments change, Darwin believed, species that were suited for the new environment could survive while others perished. Darwin used this line of thinking to explain why the fossilized remains that he collected contained animal species that no longer existed. Changing environments, Darwin believed, had allowed some organisms to thrive while others could not survive. Thus, Darwin believed, species alive today had spent millions of years evolving into their current form to fit the needs of the environment.

ral History." The skull, however, was later removed from his room by a housekeeper who simply could not stand to clean around it. This was just the start of a conflict that would grow over time.

Theodore's father encouraged his son's love of the outdoors and, despite the boy's severe asthma, urged him to spend as much time as possible outside. He also bought books for his son from the best-

At age 10, Theodore Roosevelt's love of the outdoors conflicted somewhat with his asthma.

known outdoor writers of that time. Young Theodore continued reading everything possible on the subjects of animals and birds and soon began writing his own stories about the animals he saw around his home. At the age of nine, Theodore wrote his own simple book, which he called *Natural History of Insects*. In it, he also described his observations of fish and birds.

Despite his young age and horrible spelling (throughout his life, Theodore misspelled words because of his habit of writing them out as they sounded to him), Theodore's family was very impressed with the boy's ability to describe the animals that lived around his home. Theodore wrote about the spiders that lived in the tree outside his home and described them as being "grey spotted and black" and said that the spiders could be found "in communities of about 20." Theodore also described the spiders' favorite habitat, which he found under the bark of trees: ". . . looks exactly like some cotton on the top but if you take that off you will see several small little webs, all in a 'gumble' as we children yoused [sic] to call it, each having several little occupants."

Theodore spent hours searching in the family's yard, catching specimens for his museum. Even though Theodore's father encouraged his son to study wild creatures and write down his observations, other members of the Roosevelt household grew rather unhappy with young Theodore's growing collections of living and dead creatures. Skulls, skins, dried insects, mounted birds, and living animals could be found not only in Theodore's bedroom museum but also throughout the family's home. Guests in the Roosevelt house had to be careful whenever they wanted a drink of water because Theodore often kept live snakes that he had captured in water pitchers throughout the house. On one occasion, Theodore killed a woodchuck and brought the dead animal to the family's cook, instructing her to boil the animal for 24 hours until the bones were clean for his collection. On another occasion, one of the Roosevelt housekeepers refused to wash the clothes because Theodore had tied a live snapping turtle to the washing machine.

Yet the most famous story about Theodore and his animals did not occur at the family's home but on the bus. One day, when a woman introduced herself to Theodore, he properly replied by lifting his hat. Much to the surprise and disgust of his fellow passengers, several frogs leapt out from under young Theodore's hat and landed on the passengers.

Theodore's collection eventually had to be removed from the main house. The smell alone was nearly unbearable and house

SAVING WETLAND HABITATS

Wetlands are areas of land that hold water seasonally or all year round. According to the U.S. Geological Survey (USGS), when the United States was settled in the 1600s, there were 221 million acres of wetlands across the United States, but by the mid-1980s, only 103 million acres remained. There were several reasons why the wetlands disappeared. For example, some of the land was flooded when dams were built, while other wetland areas were drained so people could raise crops or build homes on the land. The loss of wetlands can lead to several serious consequences. Wetlands provide habitat for several species, including ducks, geese, frogs, turtles, and salamanders. Each acre of wetland that is lost reduces the available space for these species to survive. Wetlands are also important because they purify water by filtering pollutants out of it. A loss of wetlands increases the amount of pollutants in ground water, which contaminates residential areas and poses potential health risks. Wetland areas are also important for controlling flood waters.

One of the best ways to protect wetlands is by educating people about their value before it is too late. By 1993, half of the workers frequently threatened to quit if Theodore's parents did not do something to slow down the steady flow of wildlife specimens that were brought into the home, both dead and alive. After a cook found a dead mouse in the icebox, it was clear to Theodore's parents that the time had come to move their son's collection away from the main house. Theodore's collection was moved to an empty room upstairs. The frozen mouse, however, was thrown out. "Oh, the loss to science!" Theodore said as the specimen was pitched out into the

The Everglades are subtropical wetlands located in southern Florida.

world's wetlands were lost. In response, countries began to protect the remaining wetlands, first by informing the public about their importance. By teaching people about wetlands conservation, we are increasing awareness about the need to protect these valuable natural areas.

weeds. He had been planning to add many measurements about the mouse to his ever-growing journal.

Theodore became an older brother in 1860 when his mother gave birth to a second boy, whom they named Elliot. Like all of the Roosevelt children, Elliot was quickly given a family nickname, in his case "Ellie" or "Nell." In 1861 another sister, Corinne, was born. She was called Conie. Theodore was very close to his two younger siblings and they frequently played together. They called themselves "We Three" and seldom played with their older sister Bamie, who tended to mother and boss the younger children. Theodore and his younger brother and sister were often joined by another girl whose father was a friend of Theodore's grandfather. Her name was Edith Kermit Carow.

Yet while Theodore's love of nature and the outdoors continued to grow, he still suffered greatly from his asthma. His struggles to breathe often woke up his parents, who held their frightened child as the boy fought for every breath. Theodore struggled with asthma attacks most often at night, gasping as he sat upright in bed. His parents continued to feed him black coffee, which actually did very little to relieve or prevent his frequent attacks. They realized that something would have to be done to stop the attacks or their worst fear might come true—that one of the attacks might actually kill him. On some nights, Theodore was so weak and breathless that he could not even blow out his own candle.

During the Civil War, Theodore Roosevelt Sr. did not serve as a soldier on the front but helped Union soldiers at their encampments by bringing them much-needed supplies and helping out wherever he could. Theodore's mother, however, had been raised in the South and her brothers were fighting for the Confederacy. This conflict between Theodore's parents became a moral issue for Theodore. He often worried about whether his actions were right or wrong and relied heavily on his father for guidance and wisdom. The good moral values that Theodore learned from his father followed him to the White House and helped direct his decision making for the rest of his life.

While his father was off to war, Theodore continued to suffer greatly from his asthma. He now had to face these attacks alone. Later in his life, he wrote that he was often afraid that he would die during these attacks and became even more frightened while his

Theodore Roosevelt called his father (*pictured here*) "the best man I ever knew."

father was away helping soldiers at the front. Still, he kept himself busy by adding to his growing museum of animals. His love of wild animals grew as he studied more and more about their habits. By the age of 11, he could draw animals very well and often kept records of the different species he had seen that day. From the many books he had read on natural history, Theodore learned to identify each species by its scientific name. For example, he knew that what most people called a woodchuck was known to scientists as *Marmota monax*, so that was the name he used.

Theodore had also learned to recognize the songs of various birds and would often identify different species he heard singing in the gardens or along New York's busy streets. "There's a wood thrush," young Theodore would say when he heard its song, and he became very excited when he heard a bird that was new to him. Once, while his mother was away visiting her relatives in the South after the Civil War had ended, she wrote Theodore a letter saying that she had seen a mockingbird. She had always encouraged her son's love of nature, and so Theodore wrote back and asked her to gather some feathers for his collection. In the same letter, he told her that he wished he could have seen the many flowers that his mother received while she was in Georgia and that he would "revel in the buggie ones." Theodore liked animals so much that he sometimes pretended to be one. For example, he was even known to read while standing on one leg like a stork.

FROM SICKNESS TO HEALTH

By the time he was 10, Theodore's museum collection had grown very large. Yet he was still suffering from asthma, and wheezing and gasping for air in the middle of the night as he sat upright in bed being held by his mother or father. Theodore was a thin boy, pale and not very athletic. He was shorter than most of his friends and he tired very easily whenever they played together.

During the 1800s, there were very few treatments for asthma sufferers like Theodore. His doctors had already prescribed coffee, which did nothing to help his breathing problems. When the war had ended, Theodore's father returned home to find that his son's condition had not improved as the boy grew older. One doctor recommended that he visit a place where the air was cooler. With that, Theodore's father decided to take him camping in the Adirondack Mountains in upstate New York. Theodore loved living so close to nature during these camping trips. During the day, he found many trails to hike and he would spend long hours examining the animal tracks he came across. He was fascinated by every species of insect and small bird he encountered. In fact, he could identify most types of birds, oftentimes by their calls alone. He was so excited to be in the woods that he often forgot about his asthma.

Still, Theodore's father continued to be very worried about his son's health. "You were born with a solid mind, but a weak body," he told his son. The only thing to do, according to him, was for his son to make his body perform as it should. Teedie's eyes lit up when he heard this advice. He loved his father and wanted him to know that he would work very hard. His father bought him a membership to a local gym, and the boy began to work out regularly. Slowly, the thin, frail, spindly-legged blonde boy became stronger, and soon, he was able to spend hours playing with other children. The asthma attacks occurred less frequently, and he could hike farther each time he and his father camped in the Adirondacks.

Theodore's father continued to encourage his son to live what he called a "vigorous life." Young Theodore began riding horses. He ran and swam in the cold waters of Oyster Bay in New York's Long Island Sound and spent hours rowing a boat. At that time, New York was still very close to the countryside, and so Theodore's father was able to teach his boys about hunting and nature. When Theodore was 12 years old, his father decided that he was old enough to hunt and bought his son a shotgun. The woods near Oyster Bay were filled with squirrels, ducks, and rabbits. In those days, families often ate wild animals, and Theodore looked forward to the opportunity to help feed his family. There was only one problem: Theodore turned out to be a terrible shot.

It was heartbreaking for Theodore not to be able to hit anything when he fired his shotgun. His friends were all far better shots than he was. As a boy, he had dreamed of hunting animals and collecting specimens for scientists and museums around the world. How could he do that if he couldn't hit what he was aiming at? As a result, his father decided to take him to the doctor once more. It did not take long to figure out what the problem was: Theodore was horribly nearsighted, which meant he could only see objects that were very close. The doctor outfitted Theodore with glasses, which were also known as spectacles. Suddenly, Theodore could see much better, and the world looked clear to him for the first time. The young man could now more closely examine the feathers of the birds and the hard outer shell of the insects that he collected.

Spectacles would become one of Theodore Roosevelt's lifelong identifying trademarks. He was always photographed and drawn by cartoonists wearing his round, rimless glasses. But life was not always easy for a boy who wore glasses. When Theodore was 14 years old, he traveled to a camp at Moosehead Lake in Maine. Traveling with him were two boys who were the same age but much bigger and stronger. They made fun of young Theodore and called him "four-eyes" because of his glasses. They picked on him constantly throughout the trip, making his life miserable. There was little he could do to fight back. In his autobiography, he explained, ". . . when I finally tried to fight them, I discovered that either one singly could not only handle me with easy contempt but handle me so as not to hurt me much and yet to prevent my doing any damage whatsoever in return."

Finally, Theodore had had enough of being bullied. When he was 14, he began to work out more frequently, running many miles and riding for hours on horseback. He spent long hours at the gym doing chin-ups, pushups, and jumping rope. His father also hired a boxing coach to teach him to box. Theodore also learned to wrestle. Although he was very slow and somewhat uncoordinated, Theodore learned how to fight and how to defend himself. Soon, working out was another favorite pastime, in addition to adding to his growing museum collection. These two activities often combined into what Theodore called a "vigorous life." When times were tough for him, he often turned to the two things that he knew he enjoyed—nature and exercise.

3

A Vigorous
Adolescence

Theodore Roosevelt loved exploring the backwoods of Oyster Bay. His detailed records of plant and animal life were impressive and often included detailed notes and measurements. But when Theodore's family decided to travel to Europe in 1869 to visit his mother's family in England, he got a chance to see totally different environments than that of Oyster Bay. The Roosevelt family traveled by boat across the Atlantic to London. From there, they traveled through France and into Switzerland where, despite his asthma, Theodore and his father climbed an 8,000-foot-high (2,438-kilometer-high) mountain. While they were in Italy, Theodore received gifts to help him with his scientific studies—a small magnifying glass, a writing stand, and a compass to help him find his way in the woods.

Travel was an important part of life to Theodore and his family. Three years after the European trip, his family set out again, this time heading for the Mediterranean Sea and, from there, on to

WHAT'S IN A NAME?

As a child, Theodore Roosevelt studied zoology, which is the study of animals. Roosevelt wanted to be a scientist and learned everything he could about the animals he studied, including their scientific name. Roosevelt knew the name of many common animals including *Marmota monax,* the scientific name for the groundhog, and *Procyon lotor*, the scientific name of the raccoon. But why, you may wonder, are animals given such complicated scientific names?

We often refer to animals by a common name, such as woodchuck, but this oftentimes causes problems. The woodchuck, for instance, is also called the groundhog or the whistle pig. In the western United States, a very close relative of the woodchuck is called the rock chuck. The bird we call a robin looks very different than the bird Costa Ricans call a robin because they are two completely different species. Common names can cause quite a bit of confusion, and for this reason, scientists avoid using them. Scientific names allow us to be more precise about a specific species of animal. The technical term for a scientific name is *binomial nomenclature*, which means "two names" in Latin. Binomial nomenclature gives each organism a genus and species name, which is similar to our first and last names. The genus is a general grouping (all big cats, for instance, are in the genus *Panthera*). Species names are specific to one individual organism. Scientific names are also taken from the Latin language because Latin is a "dead language" that does not evolve. Scientific names oftentimes tell us something about the animal, as well. For instance, the species name for the 13-lined ground squirrel

(continues)

(continued)

is *tridecemlineatus* which, in Latin, means "13 lines." Species are also divided into subspecies. Subspecies are closely related, but slightly different. Grizzlies and brown bears, for example, are the same species, but they are divided into two subspecies. Grizzlies and brown bears are both in the species *Ursus arctos*, but the grizzly subspecies is named *Ursus arctos horribilis*, or "the horrible brown bear."

Africa. Theodore was enchanted by the beautiful sandy landscape of Egypt and, as always, took careful notes of the animals that he saw as his family traveled down the Nile River: beautiful shore birds, small songbirds unlike anything he had seen in the United States, and strange insects. He was delighted by all of the wildlife he saw as his family traveled for two months down the river and into the heart of Africa. As a bonus, his asthma seldom acted up in the dry desert air.

Back home in New York, the attic of the Roosevelt home had been converted into a museum and a gym. Here, Theodore could not only add to his collection of living and dead specimens (and do so far away from the main part of the house), but he could also work out in peace. Theodore worked extremely hard to become physically fit, and his asthma attacks occurred less and less frequently. Plus, although Theodore was still a thin boy, he was growing much stronger, and his skinny legs and arms were now tightly muscled.

Theodore's favorite place, however, was Oyster Bay. The entire family enjoyed vacationing at their home there, and many of the Roosevelts later recalled how much they enjoyed their vacations by the sea. Corinne, Theodore's sister, called Oyster Bay "the happy land of woods and water." Because the Roosevelts' vacation house

At 17, Theodore Roosevelt was very active. He regularly rowed, ran, boxed, took long walks, and practiced calisthenics.

was on the coast, Theodore could observe a variety of shorebirds that he never saw near his home in the city. He also fished in the Long Island Sound and hunted in the dense forests that surrounded the bay. One time, Theodore climbed to the top of nearby Sagamore Hill and started reciting poetry loudly into the wind. Many of his best memories from childhood were of running along the deer paths and beaches of Oyster Bay in search of new specimens for his ever-growing museum collection.

During his teenage years, Theodore possessed a charm that caught the interest of various New York girls. Theodore had learned to ballroom dance and loved to take girls on long rowboat rides. He also had a good sense of humor that made him enjoyable to be around. One of the girls who attended social events with young Theodore later said, "As a young girl I remember dreading to sit next to him at any formal dinner lest I become so convulsed with laughter at his whispered sallies as to disgrace myself and be forced to leave the room." His humor and charm remained traits that Roosevelt was known for throughout his life.

THEODORE GOES TO HARVARD

Life in New York was splendid for young Theodore Roosevelt. He had many friends, enjoyed adding to his museum collection, and reading the many books that belonged to his father. Still, he could not live the life of a child forever, and Theodore's father eventually decided that he should attend college. At 16, he enrolled Theodore in Harvard, one of the finest schools in the United States.

Theodore was scheduled to begin classes in 1876. However, there was one problem: He had very little actual schooling. Although he had great factual knowledge of subjects like nature and science, he needed a great deal of help in subjects like mathematics and Latin. While Theodore continued exercising each day, he was tutored in the subjects he would need to know to be accepted by Harvard. His life became a busy combination of long hours of book work and intense periods of pushups, boxing, and gymnastics. Theodore also kept careful notes on his own physical condition, just as he had recorded the weight and measurements of the specimens in his collections. Just before entering Harvard, Theodore wrote his own measurements in his journal: "Height: 5 foot, 8 inches; weight: 124 pounds; chest: 34 inches; waist: 26 ½ inches."

When the time came to leave his family and head to Harvard in the fall of 1876, Theodore was lean and tanned from his time in the sun. Although he was still small and spoke in an excited, high-pitched voice, Theodore was in excellent shape and had passed his entrance exams with flying colors. He arrived at Harvard in Cambridge, Massachusetts, in time to prepare for his fall classes and to find a place to live. Most freshmen lived in the dormitories in the center of Harvard's campus, but the damp, cold rooms would have been very bad for Theodore's asthma. His sister Bamie, sent ahead by the family to find a house for her brother, located one near the Charles River in Cambridge, and even though Theodore would be leaving some of the comforts of his boyhood home behind, his family hired a man to tend the fire and a housekeeper for him.

Theodore did not immediately fit in at Harvard. "Harvard Men," as many of the students called themselves, acted very calm and indifferent to anything that was going on around them. They always walked with a certain strut and had an air about them that indicated that they thought they were too good for average people. Theodore did not act that way at all. While most of his classmates walked to and from classes, he ran, yelling across campus at people he knew instead of speaking quietly and politely like a good Harvard gentlemen was expected to do. While his classmates drank tea and ate lunch in silence, Roosevelt would burst into the room, shaking hands, slapping backs, and talking loudly.

However, it did not take Theodore long to win over his Harvard classmates. He had a charm and sensibility that the other boys found likeable. Theodore enjoyed sports and was eager to play, even if he was not very good. At Harvard, he continued to work out and joined the track and boxing teams. He studied hard and, on at least one occasion, became so absorbed in a book he was reading as he sat

Theodore Roosevelt, wearing his boxing gear, poses while enrolled at Harvard University circa 1880.

by the fireplace, that he did not realize his boots were on fire until he smelled the leather burning.

Roosevelt was not as big or as strong as many of the other boys at Harvard, but he worked hard and could endure pain. One of his friends, a man named Richard Welling, recalled seeing Theodore working out in the gym and was not very impressed because of his small size. Later, the two of them went ice skating with some friends on a pond not far from Cambridge on a miserably cold day. The icy winter wind was so fierce as it howled across the rough ice that none of the other boys wanted to skate. Yet Theodore did not hesitate and skated off across the ice, circling the pond in the frigid wind that blew across the landscape. As the other boys huddled together, Theodore continued skating, yelling to the others, "Isn't this bully? Isn't this bully?" Theodore was having a great time while his companions shivered and suffered. That day changed Richard Welling's opinion forever: Theodore Roosevelt was tough.

At the end of his first term, Theodore was very proud of his progress. He had taken literature, mathematics, Greek, and Latin and had made above-average grades for his class in all subjects. Studying was just one part of Theodore's hectic schedule. He went to church each morning, and then went to class, studied, and worked out. His only free time was late in the evening when he wrote letters (in fact, Theodore wrote many letters in his lifetime—at least 100,000) and continued to work on his museum. Being away at college did not stop him from enjoying his animal collection, which he added to frequently. While skinning birds and preserving already dead specimens, he also brought in many live animals. One of his friends, the captain of the football team, refused to enter Theodore's house because of the smell of the animals and the sight of the live tortoise that roamed the halls.

Despite being well liked by many of his Harvard peers, Theodore quickly realized that the people at his school had not been raised with the same beliefs that he had. Theodore's father had taught him to care for all people, especially the poor. Harvard was a school for the wealthy and elite, and very few of them had any desire to help anyone who was not like them. In contrast, during his presidency, Theodore would fight for the rights of all people everywhere. Part of the reason that he worked so hard for equality among all people was in response to the way that he saw his classmates at Harvard act. Theodore was upset by their selfish attitude. He later said that his classmates felt "no duty to join with others in trying to make things better for the many . . . ."

BIRD SONGS

Many bird-watchers can identify birds by their calls. However, did you know that birdcalls and birdsongs are two different things according to ornithologists (people who study birds)? Bird songs are longer and typically change pitch. Bird calls are shorter and are often made up of a single note. The organ that birds use to call and sing is called a syrinx, and it acts very much like a human voice box. Many bird-watchers can identify several bird species by their calls alone. Birds also have very good hearing and can even tell one bird from another just by listening to their voices the same way that humans recognize other human voices. Birds call for a variety of reasons, including to defend their territory and to contact a lost mate. Other times, birds call to demonstrate their health, to gather other birds together, or to warn of danger. Sometimes, it seems, birds just call and sing because they like to.

Parrots and parakeets are oftentimes trained to speak, and many of them have very large vocabularies. Because of their high intelligence and social nature, parrots can quickly learn to speak in words. It is not uncommon for trained parrots to have a vocabulary of more than 20 words. The world's record for the largest bird vocabulary is a parakeet that could say over 1,700 different words.

Theodore's best friend at Harvard was a boy named Henry Davis Minot. Henry shared Theodore's love of animals and could identify almost as many bird species. Together, the two hiked in the woods around Harvard and took note of the birds that they saw during each season. Theodore had brought his museum collection with him from home and also skinned and stuffed several bird specimens while at Cambridge. When the school year ended, Theodore and Henry traveled together to the Adirondacks and observed the many different species of birds that lived in the mountains. It was during this trip that Theodore heard the beautiful song of a bird called the wood thrush and later described it as "the purest natural melody to be heard in this or perhaps any land."

After their trip to the Adirondacks, Theodore and Henry began working on a four-page pamphlet titled *The Summer Birds of the Adirondacks in Franklin County, New York*. The small but well-written pamphlet described 97 species of birds that could be found in the Adirondack Mountains. Theodore enjoyed writing almost as much as he enjoyed bird-watching and, so he was thrilled when a magazine about birds gave his pamphlet a positive review. Shortly after that, he wrote *Notes on Some of the Birds of Oyster Bay, Long Island*.

A HERO LOST

The time had come for Theodore to begin deciding what his career would be. His father thought that he would go into business, but what Theodore really wanted to do was to become a naturalist and study birds and animals. Being a scientist, however, did not pay very well, and it was not at all what Theodore's father had expected his son to do. Still, Theodore Sr. also wanted his son to be happy and told young Theodore that he could become a naturalist so long as he "intended to do the very best work." Theodore signed up for classes in botany (the study of plants) and anatomy (the study of the muscles, bones, and organs that make up living things) and prepared for a life as a scientist.

During December of 1877, Theodore came home for Christmas break and found his father suffering from stomach pains. Theodore told him to take better care of himself and returned to Harvard, sure that his father would recover from his stomach pains soon enough.

However, on February 9, 1878, Theodore received a frightening message. His father was very ill again and was suffering from tremendous stomach pains. Theodore rushed home from school to be with his sick father, but he was too late. When he arrived, he found that his father had died from stomach cancer. Many of the orphans and poor children who Theodore Sr. had helped were holding a candlelight vigil outside the Roosevelt home in memory of the man who had helped so many.

The loss of his father was a crushing blow for Theodore. He was in the habit of writing long daily journal entries, but, after his father's death, he couldn't write anything for two days. "With the help of my God I will try to lead such a life as he would have wished," Theodore said in the days following. Theodore's mentor, hero, and friend was gone. The young man tried his best to stay strong despite the death of his beloved father.

In spite of his pain, Theodore tried to continue his studies at Harvard, which he believed was what his father would have wanted. The inheritance left by his father could have financed Theodore for the rest of his life, but he knew that his father would have wanted him to continue on at school "like a brave Christian gentleman," Theodore said.

To keep his mind off the loss of his father, Theodore worked very hard on his studies and kept himself busy outdoors. He often rowed his boat 25 miles (40.2 km) a day and rode his horse Lightfoot for many hours at a time. But this still was not enough to keep young Theodore's mind off the death of his father. When school ended, he left Cambridge and went to meet Bill Sewall in Maine. Sewall was a hunting and fishing guide in the wilderness of Maine, and Theodore's tutor had recommended that he take the train up to Maine and meet Bill during his summer vacation. Theodore decided that the summer following his father's death would be a good time to visit Sewall.

Theodore met Sewall at Lake Mattawankeag near the Canadian border. Bill Sewall was the kind of man that Theodore had often read about—tall, strong, and perfectly fit for a life in the northern woods. Sewall hunted, fished, and trapped in the same wilderness where bears and wolves roamed. Roosevelt instantly liked him.

Bill Sewall, however, did not have nearly as much confidence in Theodore Roosevelt. He thought that Theodore was a "thin, pale youngster with bad eyes and weak heart." Yet Theodore had a way of winning people over, and soon Sewall was impressed by the young man's desire to learn all he could about the plants and animals of the north woods. Plus, Theodore was willing to hike 25 miles a day and sleep out in the cold. He was brave in bad weather and always in good spirits. By the time Theodore returned to the train station, he and Sewall had become good friends.

INTRODUCING ALICE

Theodore Roosevelt's summer in the north woods helped him overcome his grief at the death of his father. When he returned to Harvard in the fall of 1878, he continued taking courses toward becoming a naturalist and returned to his strict workout schedule. He joined the rifle and natural history clubs and boxed often. But Theodore also had his eyes on a new prize—a thin, beautiful blonde girl named Alice Hathaway Lee, the cousin of Roosevelt's friend Dick Saltonstall. Roosevelt was so taken by Alice that, shortly after meeting her, he told a friend, "See that girl? I'm going to marry her."

However, Alice Lee did not feel the same instant attraction to Theodore. He was nice, she thought, but there were many boys who were already interested in her. Yet Theodore could not stop thinking about this beautiful girl. He frequently asked her out for walks in the woods during which he recited for her the scientific names of the various animals that lived there and described all the birds and mammals that inhabited the New England forests. Theodore wanted to marry Alice very badly, but she was young and had many suitors. Theodore was a nice young man, but sometimes he was loud and very excitable. Besides, her father, a banker from Boston, did not want his daughter to marry at such a young age.

The following summer, Roosevelt returned to Maine and set out into the wilderness again with his friend Bill Sewall. Roosevelt was growing stronger from constant exercise, and he and Bill climbed the highest mountain in Maine, Mount Katahdin. They canoed to hidden lakes, many of which did not even have names. Oftentimes, Roosevelt would have to step out and pull the canoe through the shallow, icy water but he never complained. During the final days of the trip, Bill and Roosevelt hiked more than 100 miles (160 kilometers), camping alongside the trail as they went. It rained for most of their hike, but Roosevelt was used to an outdoor life and cried out, as he often did, "Isn't this bully?"

When he returned to Harvard, Roosevelt once again set out to win the heart of Alice Lee. He thought about her often and showed up at any ball or social event she was likely to attend. Once he became so afraid that another man would ask her to marry, that he ordered a pair of dueling pistols from France.

Eventually, however, Alice agreed to marry him. His charming personality was easy to like and the couple was engaged to be married on October 27, 1880, Roosevelt's twenty-second birthday. He could not have asked for a better present—he had won the girl of his dreams.

Soon, however, Roosevelt became unhappy. While he still loved his wife and was thrilled that they were married, he was not enjoying his studies as a naturalist. He was finding out that a career as a naturalist included many boring hours working in a lab, studying specimens under a microscope, and writing down numbers, while what he really loved was being outdoors and living in the wilderness. Plus, he would have to travel to do his scientific research, which meant he would have to leave his new wife behind. The idea of being away from Alice made Roosevelt "perfectly blue."

Alice Hathaway Lee and Theodore Roosevelt are shown in 1880, the year they married.

In the spring of 1880, Roosevelt graduated from Harvard with honors. By that time, he knew that he was no longer interested in becoming a naturalist. He decided instead that he would practice law. Roosevelt was not particularly excited about being a lawyer, but it was a good, respectable business that he could conduct while living in New York with Alice. They had begun building a large, beautiful house on Sagamore Hill in Oyster Bay—the same place that Roosevelt had spent so many wonderful summers. The house would be called Leeholm in honor of Alice's family.

A Man of Politics

Theodore Roosevelt and his family had traveled to many places when he was young, but that was only the beginning. In the summer of 1880 after he graduated from Harvard, he and his brother Elliott traveled west to the plains of Iowa and Minnesota on a bird hunting trip. Roosevelt loved the wild, open grasslands of the plains and the friendly people he met there. He and his brother had an excellent time despite a bad run of luck—Roosevelt was thrown from a wagon, bitten by a snake, and both of his guns broke. Nevertheless, the American West was a place he would come to love.

Yet even this grand hunting trip could not help Roosevelt decide what he wanted to do with his life. He had a new bride and plenty of money from his inheritance, but he had no real desire to be a lawyer. Instead, he wanted to help people. At this time, the best way for someone to help the poor was to become a philanthropist, and so Roosevelt gave money to many of the same charities his father had.

ROOSEVELT BECOMES A CRUSADER

What Roosevelt really wanted to do was to go into politics. But in those days, politics was not considered a proper profession. Politicians were oftentimes crooked. It was believed that members of the upper class, such as the Roosevelts, should not be involved with people who were "brutal and unpleasant to deal with," as a family friend told Theodore.

Besides, Roosevelt had other interests, such as his passion for the outdoors. (He even climbed to the top of the Matterhorn in Switzerland on his honeymoon). He was an excellent writer and, at the age of 23, his first book, *The Naval War of 1812*, was published. Being an explorer or an author were both more acceptable in the 1880s than being a politician.

Still, Roosevelt was irresistibly drawn to politics. He began to visit Morton Hall, the headquarters for New York City's Republican Party. Soon, everyone in Morton Hall knew about the sharp, young Harvard graduate with the high voice and the toothy smile. Roosevelt wasted no time in making his feelings known. His goal was to see that the high moral standards his father had taught him were being practiced by New York politicians. Many Republicans liked Roosevelt's fire and his passion. Plus, the Roosevelt name was still very well known in New York. The other Republicans asked him to run as a Republican representative to the New York State Assembly. Roosevelt accepted the nomination, but he had only 11 days to campaign before the election. Nevertheless, on November 9, 1881, Theodore Roosevelt was elected to the New York State Assembly.

At 23, Roosevelt was the youngest member of the assembly. Yet he wasted no time and immediately began addressing the assembly about issues that he thought were important. Many of the assembly members did not know what to think of the young man with the spectacles and the big teeth. Still, it had always taken time for people to get used to Roosevelt's behavior and he knew that, sooner or later, he could win their trust.

There were many assembly members who did not like Roosevelt, though. They did not believe that a young man who had always been wealthy could understand the world of politics. Plus, they were disturbed by Roosevelt's belief in the strong moral code his father had passed down to him and his plans to bring the work of the state assembly in line with this code of good conduct. He wanted to fight against corruption, while most politicians cared more about making money for themselves and their friends than they did about common people. Roosevelt planned to change all of that.

Roosevelt saw politics as a battle of good against evil—his high moral ideas represented good and they had to defeat the evil ideas of crooked politicians all around him. Roosevelt was called a "maverick"—someone who does not do things the way they are normally done. But he didn't care what anyone called him. He simply believed that people should be treated fairly and honestly. These beliefs often strongly upset other members of the assembly. In fact, Roosevelt even kept the leg from a broken chair beside him as self-defense in case other assembly members became angry enough to physically attack him.

Other members of the state assembly warned Roosevelt that he had better begin cooperating with the important men around him. Roosevelt refused, calling them "sharks" and "swindlers." He continued to promote high moral standards and refused to be bullied by anyone. When Roosevelt spoke, everyone in the assembly wanted to hear what he had to say and they sat in perfect silence as he spoke about ending corruption and promoting good character. In February 1882, he called for the investigation of a powerful businessman on a variety of corruption charges. The rest of the assembly laughed in response, knowing that the man was so rich and powerful that he would never be investigated. Still, Roosevelt was an excellent speaker and he convinced many people that all cases of corruption should be investigated. By the spring of 1882, he had nearly enough support to go ahead with his investigation, but the accused businessman bribed enough of the other assemblymen into voting against Roosevelt's proposal, and the investigation never happened. Roosevelt was furious.

Roosevelt learned a powerful lesson during his first term in the assembly. He had met men that made laws only to benefit themselves and their friends. They reminded Roosevelt of the boys he had known at Harvard. Roosevelt realized that common people needed political officials to look out for their interests.

Roosevelt was happy when his first term ended and he could return to the life he enjoyed back at Oyster Bay. There, he often spent his time playing tennis and riding horses. Once, while on a visit to Alice's family, he pretended to be a bear while playing with some of the children. His roars and growls were so convincing that "the smaller ones began to have a horrible suspicion that perhaps I really *was* a bear."

Yet there was very little time for Roosevelt to enjoy with his wife and family before he had to return to the assembly. Once there, though, he found he was very popular and well known because of his lively personality and his passion for what he believed to be "moral battles." Several newspapers had written favorable things about young Roosevelt, and he was now a star of the Republican Party. Roosevelt was so well liked, that the other Republicans nominated him to be speaker at the state legislature, which meant that he would represent his political party in front of the assembly and the governor.

Nevertheless, Roosevelt had changed. All of his life, he had lived very comfortably. His father's business had made the Roosevelts wealthy, and he had always been able to do what he wanted. Like many upper-class people of that time period, Roosevelt had no idea of the conditions that poor workers lived in. During his first term as speaker, he visited a family of cigar makers in New York City and was shocked by what he saw: Two whole families living together in one single-room apartment. They did not speak English and seldom left their home, as they spent more than 12 hours each day rolling cigars for the wealthy. They slept in tiny beds in the corners of the room beside large piles of tobacco and food scraps.

A VISIT TO SAGAMORE HILL

When Theodore Roosevelt decided to build a home for his family, he could not imagine a better place than Sagamore Hill, where he had spent so many happy summers as a child. Roosevelt hired the architectural firm of Lamb and Rich of New York for this project and, in 1884, the plans were laid out. The home was originally called Leeholm in honor of Roosevelt's first wife, Alice. After Alice's death, Roosevelt married Edith Carow and the name of the home was changed to Sagamore Hill. Sagamore was where Roosevelt's children were born and spent their early years. The house had several floors with spacious

The North Room of the Roosevelt family home, Sagamore Hill, was decorated with the skins and mounts of animals Theodore Roosevelt killed.

rooms. Roosevelt's favorite was his gun room, where he could steal away from his family and work in peace. The gun room also served as Roosevelt's trophy room. Its walls were hung with the heads and skins of game he had brought home from his hunting trips.

While serving as president, Theodore Roosevelt and his family vacationed at Sagamore Hill. After his presidency, Roosevelt lived there until his death. Today, Sagamore House is a National Historic Site under the control of the National Park Service, which Roosevelt himself helped organize. The house is located 25 miles (40 kilometers) east of New York City and is visited by many tourists annually.

His visit to this family forever changed Roosevelt's view of common workers. He had seen firsthand just how bad the living conditions for them could be. He then decided that it was his moral obligation to do his best to help them.

Roosevelt also learned something else very important from this visit. Powerful businessmen, he discovered, would oftentimes pay employees poor wages and force them to work in poor conditions in order to increase and protect their profits. This was common practice before Roosevelt took office, and government officials, who were often backed by large corporations, did nothing to stop it. Throughout Roosevelt's political career, he worked very hard to be sure that every American was treated with dignity. He believed that the resources of the nation should be used to help improve the quality of life for the American people.

Thus, after he returned to Albany, Roosevelt immediately went on the attack against powerful, corrupt businessmen. He told state Supreme Court justices that they had done a poor job of upholding laws to protect common people because they "knew legalism, but not life." Roosevelt proposed laws to stop corrupt officials from making money while in office. Several of the bills he proposed were aimed at preventing big business from controlling the government. Most importantly to Roosevelt, he attacked the "wealthy criminal class," which was the name he gave to those businessmen who used a corrupt legal system and an immoral state government to make large amounts of money without regard for the people of New York. His speeches were long and passionate, and he frequently pounded his hand into his fist as he addressed the state assembly.

SAFARI TO THE BADLANDS

The stress of these political battles took its toll on Roosevelt. He needed some good news, and, in June 1883, he received just that when his wife Alice told him that she was going to have a baby. Roosevelt was thrilled and worked hard to finish Leeholm house on Sagamore Hill. He purchased another 95 acres (38.4 hectares) of land near Oyster Bay so that his family could enjoy the outdoors as he had when he was a child.

Meanwhile, Roosevelt continued to be very busy fighting political battles at the state capital, so when retired Naval Commander H.H. Gorringe asked Roosevelt to accompany him on a hunting trip out West, he became very excited. While they planned to hunt for deer, elk, antelope, and geese, their major goal was to kill a bison. Most of the great herds of bison that roamed across the West had been wiped out by buffalo hunters who killed the bison for their skins. However, a few herds were still to be found in their destination, the Dakota Territory.

At the last moment, Gorringe informed Roosevelt that he could not go. Roosevelt packed his gear and headed for the train station anyway. Hunting bison on the wild Dakota plains sounded bully to Roosevelt and if he had to travel alone it was fine by him.

Roosevelt arrived at the town of Little Missouri in the Badlands of the Dakota Territory, which today is in the western portion of the state of North Dakota. For thousands of years, the region had been the hunting ground of the Lakota Indian tribe until ranchers began driving cattle into the region and railroads started crossing the plains. When the first white hunters reached the plains, huge herds of bison stretched from the Rocky Mountains all the way to the Midwest, and there were no laws limiting how many could be killed. Armed with powerful rifles, the buffalo hunters had reduced the bison from several million animals to only a few hundred by the time Roosevelt reached the Badlands in 1883.

As a naturalist, Roosevelt disapproved of how these lawless hunters had killed more bison than they needed. As a child, he had read about the huge herds that had once roamed the plains. Now that he was there, he was sad to find only a few places left where they could still be hunted.

When Roosevelt arrived in Little Missouri, he was surprised by how wide and empty the plains were. With his bag on his back and his rifle case in hand, Roosevelt set out on foot across the plains to a group of buildings in the distance, where he found a small hotel at which he could stay during his hunt.

At first, Roosevelt was not well liked by the cowboys of the Dakota Territory. He was a small man who spoke very well, wore spectacles and clean, expensive clothes, and had lived most of his life in New York City. At first, no one wanted to take such a seemingly inexperienced man from the East on a hunting trip into the wild Dakota Badlands. Nevertheless, Theodore found a man named Joe Ferris who agreed to help him in his hunt for bison.

Roosevelt was amazed by the unique geography of the Badlands—its sagebrush plains that stretched for miles and its strange, pointed rock formations that appeared desolate and lifeless (and for which the Badlands are named). Hunting in these stark, featureless rock hills would have been a challenge for most easterners, but not for Roosevelt. He loved this wilderness. During the day, he hunted deer, bison, and antelope. At night, he enjoyed the clean, cool air and the stars that stretched from one horizon to the other while he listened to the wolves and coyotes that howled in the far-off hills.

Still, the Badlands were not an easy place to hunt. Roosevelt had to deal with cold and heat as well as the strong winds and dust storms that gusted across the prairie. He encountered four rattlesnakes while he hunted, one of which nearly bit him while he was stalking antelope. Had the snake not given its warning rattle, Roosevelt would have crawled right on top of it. But even though the plains were dry and dusty and the hunting very difficult, it was a grand adventure for Roosevelt. Joe Ferris soon learned that the New York boy with the funny accent and the spectacles could handle the hardships of the plains with ease.

The highlight of Roosevelt's hunt was taking his bison. While Roosevelt and Ferris were riding along the rough, rocky hillsides of the Badlands, Roosevelt saw the hoofprint of a very large bison bull. He slipped down from his horse and continued on foot until he crawled over the crest of a hill and saw the bull in a valley below, with its massive shoulder hump that was taller than Roosevelt's head.

Roosevelt took careful aim and fired, killing the huge bison. Shortly afterwards, he wrote a very excited letter to his wife Alice and told her that he would "bring you home the head of a great buffalo bull."

Roosevelt had been considering starting a business and his trip to the Dakotas helped him decide how he would invest his savings. Instead of starting a shipping company like his father had, Roosevelt bought another kind of stock—livestock. In fact, he bought a ranch and 400 head of cattle in the Badlands. He felt confident that he

THE AMERICAN BISON

The history of the bison (*Bison bison*) will always be associated with expansion in the American West. During America's colonial period, millions of bison lived in vast herds that could be found across the country. Millions of bison grazed on the open plains forming the largest herd of mammals ever found on Earth. When white settlers pushed into the West, they began killing bison in large numbers. These great herds were killed in part because their hides were very valuable and also because killing the bison would cripple the Plains Indians who relied on the animals for food.

By the late 1800s, the plains were almost devoid of bison. Buffalo hunters often shot the animals, took the skins, and left the meat behind to spoil under the hot sun. By the turn of the twentieth century, the great herds of bison had been reduced to less than a thousand animals. But conservation and careful management allowed their numbers to increase. Today, there are almost a half million bison in the United States. Many of these bison are located on private ranches and are sold for food. Bison meat is popular with many people because it is lower in fat and cholesterol than regular beef and is therefore healthier. Bison herds will never reach the could make money raising cattle on the land he called the Chimney Butte Ranch. Roosevelt also decided he wouldn't tell his wife about buying the ranch right away.

DOUBLE TRAGEDY

When Roosevelt returned to New York after his hunting trip, he immediately returned to fighting corruption in the New York State

American bison is a North American species that is also sometimes called the American buffalo, although it is not a true buffalo. They once roamed the grasslands in massive herds.

numbers found in this country before white settlement. The fact that there are any bison at all, however, is a testament to the conservation efforts of a select group of individuals who set out to preserve this species for future generations.

Assembly. His first task was to take on the New York City police department where, for years, rumors had circulated about police corruption. For example, criminals could avoid serving jail time if they could pay bribes to the police. Conditions in jails were very bad, but prisoners who could afford to pay off the guards were placed in clean, comfortable cells. Roosevelt began his attack on police corruption by efforts to pass laws that made it illegal for police to accept bribes.

Then, on February 12, 1884, Roosevelt received a telegram—his wife had given birth to a little girl. With great excitement, Roosevelt boarded the train for New York City.

However, his happiness would not last long. When he knocked on the door at his parents' home, his brother Elliott answered, looking very upset. "There is a curse on this house," Elliott said. "Mother is dying, and Alice is dying, too!"

Stunned, Roosevelt ran inside to find that his mother was dying from typhoid fever downstairs while his wife Alice was dying from kidney failure upstairs. (The baby survived and was named Alice Lee, after her mother.)

Early on the morning of Valentine's Day 1884, Mittie Roosevelt, Theodore's mother, died of typhoid fever with her sons and daughters by her bedside. Shortly afterwards, Alice, the girl that Theodore loved so much and had worked so hard to win, died in a bed not far from the room where Roosevelt kept his animal collection as a child.

Roosevelt was crushed. He felt as if his whole world had gone dark and he could barely face the pain. In his journal, he wrote, "The light has gone out of my life." Roosevelt, who was still suffering from the loss of his father a few years before, had lost his wife and his mother on the same awful day.

Roosevelt returned to Albany and tried to continue serving on the state assembly, but he could not forget about the deaths of his wife and mother. He was quickly losing hope on the political front, as well. In 1884, Grover Cleveland, a Democrat, won the presidential election for the first time since the Civil War. Roosevelt's Republican Party was no longer in control of the White House.

Finally, it all became too much for Roosevelt to bear. Feeling he could no longer continue to live in New York, Roosevelt took baby Alice to live with his sister Bamie. As he so often did during times of crisis, Roosevelt headed for the wilderness for relief from the pains of daily life. He packed his bags and left New York on a train west to the Badlands. When he arrived in Little Missouri in the Dakota Territory, he traded his job as a politician for a new career—managing the Chimney Butte and Elkhorn Ranches.

Life on the Plains

The life of a western cowboy was not easy in the 1880s. The winters were cold and brutal. Frigid winds brought heavy snow down from Canada that buried the plains in high, white drifts. When the snow thawed, the plains became a sea of sloppy mud. With so few trees, mudslides were common because the roots of the grass did not go deep enough to hold the ground in place when it rained. Summers were very hot and there was not much shade on the grassy plains. Sudden severe thunderstorms, sometimes accompanied by tornadoes, ripped across the prairie.

Ranchers and cowboys had to work outside in all these conditions as they tended large herds of cattle. Most of these men were not well educated and did not have very much money. There were gunfights, and groups of angry ranchers would chase cattle thieves and kill them, sometimes without a trial.

ROOSEVELT, THE DAKOTA RANCHER

With their hard lifestyle, many Dakota cowboys were shocked when they met ranch owner Theodore Roosevelt. When he stepped down off the train in Little Missouri, he was dressed in a custom-made leather shirt with long, leather fringe hanging down from the arms. Like many of the other cowboys, he also carried a large hunting knife but there was one major difference—Roosevelt's knife was studded with jewels and had been handmade by the famous jeweler Tiffany & Co. of New York.

Roosevelt's clothes set him apart from the other cowboys on the Dakota plains, but the biggest difference was in the way he spoke. Most of the cowboys spoke with gruff, smoky voices and used poor grammar. Many of them chewed tobacco and had brown stains running down their mouths and beards. Roosevelt had been raised and educated in a wealthy New York home. He learned to speak correctly and had attended Harvard.

Even though the cowboys often teased Roosevelt about his clothes, his fancy speech, and his spectacles, they all came to respect him. In the dead of winter, or the blistering heat of summer, Roosevelt worked alongside them without complaint. He was not afraid of outlaws, rattlesnakes, wolves, or storms. He was no longer a sickly boy who suffered and wheezed at night, too weak to blow his own candle out. He was now very strong, with broad shoulders, thick arms and a big, broad chest. He carried a pistol and a rifle, and he knew how to use both of them, although Roosevelt himself admitted he was not a very good shot. All the cowboys soon learned that the man with the funny accent, spectacles, and big, toothy smile was as tough as any of them.

In one famous story that illustrates his toughness, Roosevelt once stopped in at a saloon in Montana after a day spent working on his Chimney Butte Ranch. As he came through the doors, he noticed that the other customers were being terrorized by a madman who was standing at the bar with both of his pistols drawn. Roosevelt

THE BADLANDS

The Badlands of North and South Dakota are some of the most unique geographical features in the United States. The rock formations that make up the Badlands vary in color from very light gray to almost black. Each year, visitors to the Badlands marvel at the variety of colors that make up these weird geographic features. But what makes the Badlands so colorful? When the area was formed over 70 million years ago, it was actually covered by a shallow ocean that stretched across much of the Great Plains. Sedimentary rock fossilized in the Badlands and still contains the fossils of many marine animals. Over the next 70 million years, a variety of different sediments settled in layers onto the Badlands areas. These sediments give the walls of the Badlands their layered appearance.

Scientists and visitors alike are amazed by the number of fossilized organisms from different periods in Earth's history that can be found in the different sedimentary layers. In the Badlands, the prehistory of the American West is preserved in its fossil beds. Once these beds had formed, water slowly carved them into the rock walls that we see today. The erosion caused by these flowing rivers also created a series of different channels. Rainwater still continues its work in the Badlands as it washes away the surface of the rock bit by bit.

ignored him and sat down in the corner. Soon, the madman took note of Roosevelt, who he called "four eyes," and ordered him to buy everyone a drink. After looking around the room at the terrified faces, he agreed that he would buy a round. He then stood up and walked toward the bar, but at the last minute he took three rapid swings at the man, hitting him in the jaw and knocking him flat on his back. The sheriff was then called in to arrest the drunken cowboy.

Roosevelt loved life on the plains. It was very different than anything he had ever known in New York City. No one cared what family you came from or how rich you were. None of the cowboys knew that Roosevelt had been a rich, sickly child spoiled by two adoring parents. They knew him simply as "Teddy," the four-eyed owner of the Chimney Butte and Elkhorn Ranches, the man who smiled often, laughed loudly, and who could write and speak well but who could also do cowboy work day and night. During one spring roundup, Roosevelt split his time between driving cattle and reading the popular novel *War and Peace* by the Russian writer Leo Tolstoy. The book was very long—more than 1,000 pages—but Roosevelt finished it by the end of the roundup.

At the end of the work day, Roosevelt and his men rode back to his ranch house on the banks of the Little Missouri River. There, they would sit in rocking chairs on the porch and read books until the sun went down. At night, they sat inside by the big fireplace and played checkers or talked until they fell asleep. Occasionally, they heard strange sounds in the night and awoke in the morning to find that the pack rats that lived behind holes in the walls had stolen their belongings. One of the larger pack rats even carried off a pistol.

The life of a prairie cowboy was always busy and full of danger. The busiest times of the year were the spring and fall roundups, when cowboys set out across the plains to gather all of the cattle, including their newborn calves, and also to inspect the older cows to be sure that none of them were sick. But the cowboy's workload was not limited to the spring and fall. During the rest of the year, there were still horses to break for riding, sick cattle to doctor, buildings to repair, water to gather, and herds to protect from marauding wolves, cougars, and cattle thieves.

As busy as he was, Roosevelt could not resist becoming involved in politics, even all the way out on the lone prairie. He served as a deputy sheriff and was a founding member of the Little Missouri Stockman's Association, a group that helped make laws for Dakota ranchers and helped stop cattle theft. Roosevelt also wrote a good deal during this time, completing three books about his adventures on the Dakota plains: *Hunting Trips of a Ranchman* (1885), *Ranch Life and the Hunting Trail* (1888), and *The Wilderness Hunter* (1893). Readers in the eastern United States were thrilled by Roosevelt's true stories of western life with its wide-open spaces and wild characters. And because he was a trained scientist, his books also described the plants and the insects as well as the larger animals of

INVASIVE SPECIES

Invasive species are plants and animals that are introduced into an area where they do not naturally occur. Oftentimes, humans are responsible for these introductions, either intentionally or by accident. Introducing species that are not native to the area creates a host of problems. Many species, like the Asian carp, reproduce very quickly and crowd out native species of fish. Nonnative plants that are often introduced into people's yards for decoration can quickly spread into the local habitat and pose a threat to other plants and wildlife. One invasive plant that has caused serious problems in the southern United States is kudzu, a Japanese vine introduced to reduce soil erosion. After it was introduced, this vine quickly spread throughout the environment and overwhelmed local species, completely blanketing local plants, trees, and even buildings with its long, thin, green vines.

Exotic pet owners in and around Florida's Everglades National Park have created a serious invasive species problem there as well. Burmese pythons, large snakes from Asia that are similar to boas and anacondas, are oftentimes released into the park when owners no longer want them. The habitat in Florida is perfect for pythons, which eat native species and compete with other native species, dramatically changing the ecosystem.

the plains. Roosevelt's books were very popular, and he became one of the best-known western writers.

Roosevelt also often wrote about one of the major problems facing plants and animals in the West: overgrazing. During the 1880s, raising cattle and selling the beef at the stock markets in Chicago was a way of becoming wealthy. Badlands ranchers knew that the more cattle they raised, the more money they could make, so they kept as many cows as possible, with the result that their herds ate most of the grass. This was very hard on the other grazing animals that lived on the plains. Deer, antelope, elk, and bison were forced to leave the overgrazed prairies and either died out or moved up into the mountains. Predators like wolves and grizzly bears followed the grazing herds because that was their only food source. Soon cattle and horses became the only large herbivores on much of the Dakota prairie.

Roosevelt became greatly concerned about overgrazing and tried to convince his fellow ranchers that they must limit the amount of damage their cattle did to the prairie's ecosystem. The grassy plains, which had been so healthy and green only a few years before, were quickly being eaten away by the livestock. To make matters worse, huge herds of sheep were introduced to the area during this time. While cattle-grazing kept the prairie grass very short, sheep actually ate the grass all the way down to the roots and killed it. Sheep-grazing was even more destructive to the plains than cattle-grazing. Roosevelt knew that if ranchers did not reduce their large numbers of cattle so that the grass could grow back, the prairie might never recover.

ROOSEVELT AND THE GRIZZLY

Roosevelt hunted often during his time on the plains. Sometimes he hunted for sport, but more often he hunted to feed the many ranch hands who worked for him at the Chimney Butte and the Elkhorn. He mostly hunted ducks, grouse, and rabbits and oftentimes caught trout. Once in awhile, he managed to bring down a larger animal, like a deer, antelope, or bighorn sheep. During the cold winter months, blankets made from bear and bison hides were essential for staying warm.

Yet there was one animal that Roosevelt wanted to hunt most of all—the largest predator in the West: the grizzly bear. Grizzlies stood nearly eight feet (2.4 meters) tall and weighed more than a thousand pounds and had no predators besides man. Even a hunter armed with a rifle stood a good chance of being attacked, or even killed, when encountering a grizzly.

Grizzlies had been wiped out on the plains, but they were still a threat to hunters like Roosevelt who traveled into the Bighorn and Bitterroot mountain ranges, which are located in part of Montana as well as in Wyoming and Idaho, respectively. Once, Roosevelt went hunting in Montana with a guide he called Hank, a mean old man who suffered from arthritis and was so rude that Roosevelt finally left him behind with most of their supplies and went on alone. Toward evening, Roosevelt found a quiet camping spot in the mountains where he could spread his buffalo-skin sleeping bag on a pile of pine branches. Yet he was also hungry and the sun was setting fast: If he wanted any meat for dinner, he would have to hunt for it.

Roosevelt hoped to bring back a grouse or a deer for his dinner, but instead he found something much larger after he crested a hill overlooking a valley ringed with pine trees. There, in an open, grassy patch on the hillside, was a very large male grizzly.

The bear was unaware that Roosevelt was nearby and continued feeding. Roosevelt took aim with his Winchester rifle and squeezed the trigger. The bear roared and ran into a thicket with Roosevelt close behind. Roosevelt ran like a madman, stooping and standing on his tiptoes, hopping to finish the bear off quickly so that it would not suffer. As he emerged from the thicket, he saw the huge grizzly standing in another clearing and fired once again.

Roosevelt figured that his second shot would drop the bear, but it did not. Instead, the grizzly turned toward Roosevelt, let out a long growl, and rushed at him.

Roosevelt had little time to react. The bear disappeared into some trees for a moment and when it reappeared, it was very close, charging at full speed with its jaws open and teeth bared. Roosevelt fired again, but the shot did not even slow the bear down. Finally, the bear was on top of him just as he fired his fourth and final shot—so close, Roosevelt had to dive to one side to avoid the swipe of the bear's outstretched paw. Roosevelt pulled four more cartridges from the leather loops of his belt with one hand, reloaded his rifle, and spun around . . . only to find that the bear had finally died.

Stories like the one about his Montana grizzly hunt, which he told in his book *The Wilderness Hunter*, made Roosevelt famous back East. His friends in New York could only imagine the adventurous life that Roosevelt was living on the prairie. The small, sickly boy they once knew had turned into a champion of the wilderness, a man who could shoot down charging grizzlies and drive cattle through the stormy Dakota winters. Roosevelt himself admitted later in life that without the toughness he developed during his time as a rancher, he never would have had the strength needed to become president of the United States.

IN PURSUIT OF OUTLAWS

One spring morning, Roosevelt and his men awoke to discover that a boat of Roosevelt's, which was normally tied to a cottonwood tree along the Little Missouri River, just outside the ranch house, had been stolen. Roosevelt immediately suspected his neighbor Mike Fennigen of committing the theft. Roosevelt had learned never to back down from a challenge. If word got out that Roosevelt and his men on the Elkhorn Ranch put up with thieves, soon others would come to steal from them. Roosevelt wanted justice and made plans to catch Fennigen himself. Roosevelt and his friends, Will Dow and Bill Sewall (who moved to the Badlands to work with Roosevelt after they met in Maine) set out in another wooden boat after Fennigen. It was March 1886, and the Little Missouri River was still running with ice along both shores. The ride was cold and treacherous, but Roosevelt and his companions braved the large ice floes and fallen trees as they navigated down the river. Falling into the fast and icy Little Missouri meant almost certain death. Nevertheless, Roosevelt and his cowboys kept up their pursuit.

After traveling downstream for some time, they found their boat tied up on the bank of the river. They saw smoke rising up through the trees and knew this meant that the thieves were nearby. Roosevelt steered his boat onto shore and snuck up to the camp with his men.

Just as Roosevelt figured, they had caught up with Fennigen, along with two other men, named Burnsted and Pfaffenbach. Roosevelt, Dow, and Sewall captured them by surprise and held them at gunpoint. Usually in the Dakota of the 1880s, thieves were hung on the spot, and Roosevelt could legally have killed all three of them, but he decided to take them back alive to Little Missouri to face the justice they deserved. But there was one problem—taking the men back would require another perilous boat ride up the river.

Still, they made it back. Upon their return to town, Roosevelt allowed Dow and Sewall to go on home to the ranch and marched the three thieves into town by himself, walking 10 feet (3 meters) behind them across the muddy prairie with his gun cocked and ready. Fennigen was sentenced to three years in jail for his crime. Roosevelt received a reward of $50 for capturing the outlaws.

By 1886, Roosevelt's worst fears had come true. The beautiful green prairie, once a sea of brilliant grass, had been reduced to dust by the huge herds of cattle and sheep. The plains of the Dakotas had been poorly managed—in their desire to become rich by selling beef, the other ranchers had brought in far more cattle than the prairie would hold. With the grass almost completely gone, the ranchers had nothing to feed their huge cattle herds.

To make things worse, the loss of grass meant that there was nothing to hold the soil in place. As a result, the plains faced new threats. If the summer was dry, the soil would turn to dust, and with no grass to hold it in place, the hot summer winds might blow away the topsoil, turning the prairie into a lifeless desert.

Roosevelt had warned his fellow ranchers about the consequences of their greed. Now, there were so many cattle that the

This 1886 portrait of Theodore Roosevelt shows him as he was campaigning as the Republican candidate for mayor of New York City.

price of beef dropped. After Bill Sewall and Will Dow took a herd by train to sell in Chicago, they received so little payment for the cows that they lost money on the trip.

Meanwhile, Roosevelt had been thinking about home more often. While he was a rancher, he had returned to New York for a visit and amazed his friends and family with the stories he told them of life in the West. During this visit, Roosevelt, now a well-known western hunter and writer, tried his hand at fox hunting. The popular method of hunting fox at this time was for the hunting party to ride on horseback behind a pack of dogs that chased the fox until they caught up with it. Roosevelt loved the excitement of the hunt and gladly joined in until his horse fell while trying to jump a fence and rolled over him. He broke his arm, but true to his image as a tough man, Roosevelt continued the hunt and actually stayed with the party until the end. When his daughter Alice saw her father with his broken arm and scratched face, she was so upset, she refused to even give him a hug.

In 1886, Roosevelt told his good friends Bill Sewall and Will Dow that he was not going to be a rancher any longer. The plains had been virtually ruined by too much cattle-grazing, and Roosevelt could not bear to witness the end of the world he loved so much. Besides, he had decided it was time to give politics another try.

When Roosevelt returned home, he was immediately asked by the New York Republican Party to run for mayor of New York, which he agreed to, even though he knew he was bound to lose. The Democrats had a strong lead and he entered the race very late. Even though he lost the election, Roosevelt was now the hero of New York's Republican Party. He had been well liked before he became a rancher. Yet, by 1886, after publishing three successful books and living the life of a Wild West cowboy, Roosevelt was a star.

After the 1886 election, Roosevelt set sail for England. There, shortly after arriving, and much to the surprise of almost everyone who knew him, Roosevelt married his childhood friend Edith Carow on December 2, 1886. The wedding was very quiet, and few people knew that Roosevelt had even been speaking with Edith.

Edith Roosevelt poses for a portrait.

She had visited him after he broke his arm on the fox hunt, and the two became good friends again. When Roosevelt returned to North Dakota afterward, he and Edith wrote letters to each other. They had kept their engagement a secret because Roosevelt did not want people to think he had forgotten about his first wife Alice. In fact, Roosevelt was haunted by the death of Alice for many years. It bothered him so much that he never spoke about her to his daughter Alice and never mentioned her in his autobiography, which he published years later.

Roosevelt and Edith were very happy together. They had been good friends since childhood. She knew all about his love of the outdoors and he knew about her bad temper, but they enjoyed each other's company and would spend the rest of their lives as husband and wife.

When the couple finally returned to America after the wedding, Roosevelt had finally decided what he wanted for a career: He was ready to be a politician.

A Rough Rider
in Washington, D.C.

When the Roosevelts returned to Oyster Bay after a four-month honeymoon, Edith was pregnant with their first child. It was during this time that Roosevelt changed the name of the house on Oyster Bay from Leeholm to Sagamore Hill.

Bad news was also waiting when Roosevelt returned. The winter of 1886 to 1887 was very bad and blizzards buried the Badlands in heavy ice and snow. Cattle were dying by the thousands, including the stock of the Chimney Butte and Elkhorn ranches. Many of the men who worked on Roosevelt's ranches left the Badlands when the weather became too severe. Only a handful of men remained to tend to the starving cattle. Roosevelt wound up losing a huge amount of money.

While Edith redecorated the house, Roosevelt worried about his finances. To continue living at Sagamore Hill, he had to find a job that paid well enough to support his family. Roosevelt spent several months writing about his adventures out west and his books were

The Roosevelt family home, Sagamore Hill, is located in Oyster Bay, Long Island, New York, where Theodore Roosevelt spent much of his time as a child.

well liked by readers and reviewers. On September 13, 1887, Edith gave birth to their first son, whom his father named Theodore Roosevelt Jr. Soon after the birth of his son, Roosevelt's daughter Alice, whom he had seen very little since he left for the plains, moved in with the family at Sagamore Hill.

FIRST STEPS TOWARD CONSERVATION

In the fall of 1887, Roosevelt returned on a hunting trip to his Badlands ranches and found that his worst fears had come true. The prairie, once a wide sea of tall grass that stretched from horizon to horizon, had been grazed to virtually nothing by the cattle and sheep that had survived the winter storms. The grasslands had been replaced by a wide, dry landscape that held virtually no game. Greedy ranchers had all but ruined the vast prairie.

When he returned home to New York, Roosevelt spoke to his friend George Bird Grinnell, who was the editor of the magazine *Forest and Stream*. Both men agreed that if America's wildlife was not protected, overgrazing and overhunting would decimate game populations across the country, resulting in the loss of habitat and the extinction of many species. Roosevelt had already seen the bison, which once roamed the prairies in huge herds, reduced nearly to extinction. Together, Roosevelt and Grinnell founded the Boone and Crocket Club, an organization comprised primarily of hunters who were concerned by the loss of wild game and by habitat loss. Boone and Crockett, which still exists today, became a very important voice in the conservation movement because many of its members were politicians and businessmen. Roosevelt became the club's first president.

Roosevelt's first mission as Boone and Crockett president was to stop companies from building in Yellowstone National Park, which was established in 1872. Lodges and clubs were set to be built within the park's boundaries and a railroad was proposed that would run directly through the park. Roosevelt and the Boone and Crockett Club managed to stop companies from building inside the park. Congress agreed with Roosevelt that the public land should be preserved and passed the Park Protection Act. After saving much of Yellowstone, Roosevelt went to Congress to ask them to slow the destruction of western forests by timber companies.

Roosevelt enjoyed his time working with the Boone and Crockett Club, but he needed to find a job that paid well enough to support him and his family, and so he started writing a series of books entitled *The Winning of the West*, which he divided into four volumes.

IS HUNTING CONSERVATION?

One of Theodore Roosevelt's favorite pastimes was hunting. Yet Roosevelt is known as a pioneering conservationist. How is this possible?

Theodore Roosevelt started the Boone and Crockett Club to bring hunters together in an effort to protect wildlife for future generations. Several other groups with similar goals have emerged since Roosevelt's time. Ducks Unlimited, an organization founded by waterfowl hunters, helps maintain healthy wetlands ecosystems. Other hunter-driven groups such as the Rocky Mountain Elk Foundation, Safari Club International, and the National Wild Turkey Federation help support wildlife and maintain habitat. Hunters spend more than $4 billion each year, much of which goes to state and national agencies that oversee wildlife management.

In 1937 the Pittman-Robertson Act went into effect. The act provides money for state wildlife agencies from a tax on the sale of items related to hunting. In the past, profits from this act have helped fund many wildlife restoration projects. Hunters for the Hungry is a program that provides meat from animals that hunters kill to food shelters. In 2009, Hunters for the Hungry provided one-and-a-half-million servings of food to Virginia residents alone. Roosevelt's legacy as a hunter and conservationist lives on today through the members of these groups.

A POLITICIAN'S RISE

It was not long, however, before Roosevelt returned to politics. The Republican Party wanted him to speak on their behalf against Democrat Grover Cleveland's proposition to lower tariffs on goods imported from other countries. Roosevelt traveled around the Midwest, giving fiery speeches that caught the public's attention. Voters were impressed by this outspoken man who had lived as a cowboy on the prairie. Roosevelt enjoyed speaking to crowded audiences and his fame spread across the country. Everyone wanted to hear his passionate words about American morality and commerce.

With Roosevelt's help the Republican Party drew support. Roosevelt used his growing popularity to help convince his friend Henry Cabot Lodge, a senator from Massachusetts, to help him gain a position in the Republican Party. President Benjamin Harrison agreed that Roosevelt deserved a job in Washington D.C. and named Roosevelt as the U.S. civil service commissioner in 1888.

As civil service commissioner, Roosevelt was responsible for maintaining the civil rights of government workers. Until Roosevelt arrived, the position was something of a joke. Politicians wanted to be sure that they could appoint and hire anyone they wanted and so the civil service overlooked hiring violations. Roosevelt, however, immediately began attacking agencies that he felt did not offer equal employment opportunities to all Americans. Roosevelt immediately went after the New York Customs House for their hiring practices and began giving speeches about the equal rights of all workers across the Midwest. The people and the press loved Roosevelt's passion and desire to stamp out immorality in government, but politicians who had always enjoyed having their own way did not like Roosevelt's aggressive style.

When Democrat Grover Cleveland was elected President again in 1892, Roosevelt was sure he would be fired. But Cleveland liked Roosevelt's style despite the fact that Roosevelt was a Republican and allowed him to stay on as commissioner. Roosevelt was delighted and continued working hard to be sure that fair hiring practices were upheld for each government position. Anyone who challenged Roosevelt's moral authority was prone to receive a tongue lashing or, if they continued to ignore his requests, be sanctioned by the government.

In 1889, Roosevelt's wife Edith gave birth to Kermit, the couple's second child. Two years later the Roosevelts had a daughter that

Theodore Roosevelt poses in 1895 with (*left to right*) son Archie, son Theodore Jr., daughter Alice (from his first marriage), son Kermit, second wife Edith Carow Roosevelt, and daughter Ethel. Two years later, another son, Quentin, was born.

they named Ethel. In 1894, Edith gave birth to the couple's fourth child, a boy named Archibald. By now there were five children in the home including Alice, and Roosevelt could not have been more excited. He loved his children very much and played with them often, sometimes telling ghost stories and screaming at the end to scare the children who howled in excitement. Whenever possible, Roosevelt took them into the countryside so they could camp and enjoy nature as he had done as a child. This happiness was shattered, though, when he received news that his brother Elliott, a long-time alcoholic, had died.

By 1894, the people of New York had become very excited by Roosevelt's commitment to them and his no-nonsense moral platform. He was asked to run for mayor of New York but refused, believing that pursuing the position was not a wise career move.

Roosevelt continued as civil service commissioner until 1895 when he accepted the position of president of the Board of New York City Police Commissioners from New York Mayor William Strong. It wasn't long before police officers in New York realized that Theodore Roosevelt meant business. He fired Police Superintendent Thomas Byrnes and began work to centralize the police offices. Roosevelt saw many things that he did not like in the police department and set out to change department policies. He increased the number of women who were hired as police officers and tried to stop all forms of police corruption. At that time, police officers provided their own guns, and many of them had very little training in firearms use. Roosevelt gave all police officers the same type of gun and made sure that they were trained in how to handle firearms. Many of the policies that Roosevelt enacted during his time as police commissioner later spread throughout New York and eventually across the country.

His work as police commissioner required Roosevelt to spend long hours at his office. Even after his shift ended, he would walk the streets of New York in disguise and look out for police officers who were sleeping on the job, taking bribes, or otherwise breaking the codes the police commission had set forth. Under Roosevelt's watch, the police department transformed into a well-trained, highly organized group.

Roosevelt made many enemies while he was police commissioner. Crooked police, dirty politicians, and crime bosses all wanted to get him out of New York. Roosevelt himself desired to move up in politics to a position that would make him powerful in the country at large. In particular, he had his eye on a position that would place him in charge of one of the largest fighting forces in the world: secretary of the navy.

Years before, Roosevelt had written a book about the War of 1812 that many people thought was the best book written on the subject. Even though he had no military experience, Roosevelt was a student of war and his detailed descriptions in *The Naval War of 1812* proved that. Furthermore, as secretary of the navy, Roosevelt would have the power of the U.S. Navy at his command. It seemed to be a perfect fit.

In 1896, President Harrison was replaced by another Republican: William McKinley. McKinley was a quiet man from Ohio who did not completely trust Roosevelt's fiery temper. McKinley had heard about Roosevelt's boldness and his growing popularity across the country, but he was hesitant to appoint such a hot-tempered man to a position with such power. Yet Roosevelt's friend Henry Cabot Lodge stepped in again, advising McKinley that Roosevelt would make an excellent choice for secretary of the navy. Roosevelt promised, in return, that he would keep his temper in check.

Roosevelt was named assistant secretary of the navy by William McKinley in 1897. He served under John D. Long, who was secretary of the navy and the man who would have to keep Roosevelt's passion and fire under control. (That same year, the Roosevelts had another child, a boy named Quentin.)

Roosevelt made his first appearance as assistant navy secretary on board the battleship *Iowa*. The *Iowa* was a massive ship, larger than anything else in the navy and capable of producing tremendous firepower. Roosevelt was amazed by the navy's impressive weaponry. He watched from the deck as the *Iowa* began firing its massive guns to hit targets nearly 2 miles (3.2 km) away.

It was not long before Roosevelt made his future plans for the navy known to his superiors. Roosevelt thought that the United States should continue to expand the navy and that larger warships with even more firepower than the *Iowa* should be added to the fleet. He was the first to consider submarines for military use, and thought that they would be excellent additions to the naval battery, allowing U.S. soldiers to slip into enemy waters undetected. Roosevelt believed that there were times when it was necessary and honorable for a country to go to war. He also believed that the United States should control the Western Hemisphere, driving out other

Theodore Roosevelt is shown in 1897, when he held the post of assistant secretary of the Navy.

colonial forces like the Spanish. Roosevelt would later describe his foreign policy as "big stick," which was taken from a favorite African proverb of his that stated, "Walk softly but carry a big stick." The battleship *Iowa* and its counterparts were big sticks indeed.

Secretary Long spent much of his time away from Washington at his farm in Massachusetts. Roosevelt was very happy when Long was absent because this allowed him to take over Long's duties as

NATIONAL FORESTS VERSUS NATIONAL PARKS

Theodore Roosevelt established 150 national forests and worked hard to protect America's national parks. There are distinct differences between national parks and national forests.

National parks are areas that are almost completely protected. They are supposed to remain "unimpaired for future generations" according to the National Parks Service, the organization that controls the national parks in the United States, under the direction and regulation of the Department of the Interior. National parks have very strong regulations regarding what can and what cannot happen inside of their boundaries. Logging and cattle ranching are not allowed and game populations are controlled by the park authority.

National forests have different regulations. This country's national forests are controlled by the U.S. Department of Agriculture. Unlike national parks, which are strictly controlled and highly regulated, national forests are open to more activities. Timber harvesting, hunting, firewood collection, and ranching are all permitted within the national forests under the careful control of the United States Forest Service (USFS). National parks and national forests both serve to protect and preserve America's wild lands but do so in different ways.

secretary of the navy. During a dinner with William McKinley, Roosevelt told the president of events taking place in the Caribbean island of Cuba where violent fighting was occurring between Spanish soldiers and Cubans.

The Cuban situation was much like the one the United States faced when it fought with England during the American Revolution. Yet Roosevelt had other reasons for encouraging the president to start a war with Spain. Roosevelt wanted to take away Spanish lands in the Western Hemisphere so that the United States would stand as the single colonial power in the region. Roosevelt also believed that a naval battle with Spain would be the perfect way to show the world the power of the U.S. Navy.

McKinley did not show much interest in Roosevelt's plan. Neither did Secretary Long, who returned from Massachusetts and found that his assistant had been beating the war drum during his absence. Long suffered through daily speeches that Roosevelt gave about the many reasons to go to war, plans and methods of attack, and the future benefits that would come from fighting Spain. Long was sure that Roosevelt must have spent many nights without sleep devising his plans and that he "spoiled 20 pages of good writing paper" each day.

THE ROUGH RIDERS

Still, the United States was moving toward war with Spain despite Long's objections. On February 15, 1898, the battleship *Maine*, which had been resting at port in Havana, Cuba, was blown up and 266 of the 354 soldiers on board were killed. Because of this incident, it was decided that the time had come for the United States to make a decision regarding war with Spain. There would be no more peace talks in an effort to avoid war.

It looked as though Roosevelt would get the war he so desperately wanted. Still, he also had problems to deal with at home. Edith had been very ill since Quentin's birth the previous year and had been running a fever for weeks. Roosevelt was terribly afraid she

Theodore Roosevelt poses on horseback in his Rough Riders uniform in this 1898 image.

would die as Alice had. While he was dealing with his wife's illness, he also had to contend with his daughter Alice's rebellious behavior. To deal with this, he sent Alice back to New York to live with his sister Bamie while he tended to his wife and prepared the navy for war.

Roosevelt's wish was granted by President McKinley on April 19, 1898, when the United States declared war on Spain and the U.S. Navy was prepared to be deployed for battle. By then, Edith had managed to recover from her persistent fever, so Roosevelt could focus entirely on the impending battle between the American forces and the Spanish army.

Once the war had started, Roosevelt turned his attention to another goal. He believed that a man's bravery could not be tested until he had been in a war. Because of this, and perhaps because he felt some shame that his father chose not to fight in the Civil War, Roosevelt set out to have himself appointed as commander of an armed regiment. Yet because he had no military experience, Roosevelt could not be named as a colonel. Instead, he was named assistant colonel of the 1st U. S. Volunteer Cavalry under the command of Colonel Leonard Wood.

Roosevelt's volunteers met in San Antonio, Texas, to receive their basic training in May 1898. These "Rough Riders," as they were called, came from every walk of life. Among them were New York socialites who had grown up much as Roosevelt had. Some of the men were cowboys from the prairie, men who had known Roosevelt when he lived in the Dakotas. Athletes, policemen, and businessmen also came to sign up to fight with Roosevelt in Cuba.

The Rough Riders made their way to Tampa, Florida, and then boarded the ship *Yucatan* and spent six days passing through the Gulf of Mexico before reaching the Cuban coastline on June 22, 1898, where Roosevelt saw "high, barren looking mountains rising above the shore." The ship was unable to take the men close to shore, so they had to jump down into smaller boats with their gear. Horses were pushed over the side of the *Yucatan* and swam desperately to shore before being caught by their riders. The beach was barren and desolate. Ahead of the men were miles of the thick, bug-infested tropical jungle. If Roosevelt wanted to test himself, he had found just the place to do it.

The Rough Riders made their way to the top of a large hill and camped. In the morning, Roosevelt spent time examining the birds and insects of the island, most of which he had never seen before. But he had very little time to enjoy nature. The Spaniards were waiting for American troops in the hills, ready with their Mauser to open fire when the American forces appeared below. The battle would soon commence.

Roosevelt and the Rough Riders had been on the island for about a week before plans were made to attack the hills around the town of Santiago. Wood was promoted to brigadier general and Roosevelt,

In this 1898 image, Colonel Roosevelt and his Rough Riders pose atop of a hill they captured in the Battle of San Juan.

having proven capable of leading the Rough Riders, was promoted to colonel.

On July 1, 1898, Roosevelt and his men were moving through a valley near Santiago when the Spanish began firing down on them from the hill above. Roosevelt mounted his horse and began charging up the hill with his men behind him. The Spanish forces fired down into the Rough Riders and Roosevelt's men suffered many casualties. As the Mauser bullets whistled by, the Rough Riders slashed their way through the green tangles of the Cuban forest. Roosevelt charged on up the hill as his men fell all around him.

Once he had crested the hill, Roosevelt gathered his remaining men and tried to determine where the Spanish snipers were shooting from. With his floppy hat pulled back and sweat-soaked neckerchief pulled to the side, Roosevelt closely watched an opposite ridge until he saw one of the Spaniards. Without a moment's hesitation, Roosevelt gave charge with his Rough Riders following right behind. Though the Spaniards were in trenches dug into the mountainside, they were overwhelmed by the Rough Riders and Colonel Roosevelt and driven off the mountain. Soon after, the Spanish forces pulled out of Santiago and headed back for Spain. Roosevelt not only got the war he wanted, but he was a hero, and the battle resulted in the United States winning the Spanish-American War, which reduced Spanish influence in the Western Hemisphere.

A NEW AMERICAN HERO

Roosevelt enjoyed a hero's welcome when he reached New York aboard the battleship *Miami*. For his bravery in battle, Roosevelt was awarded the Congressional Medal of Honor and became an even bigger celebrity in his home state. Many people asked the former Harvard graduate, Wild West cowboy, and war hero to consider running for governor of New York. Roosevelt wondered whether or not this was a good idea. He was only 40 years old, and if he won the election to be governor, he would most likely be considered as a presidential candidate. However, 40 was a very young age to be

FOR GOVERNOR·   FOR LIEUT·GOVERNOR

COL·THEODORE ROOSEVELT·   TIMOTHY L·WOODRUFF·

An 1898 campaign poster advertises a uniformed Theodore Roosevelt for New York Governor and Timothy L. Woodruff for lieutenant governor.

running for president of the United States. If he won, he would be the youngest president ever.

Roosevelt could not pass up on his chance to be elected governor, and, in 1898, he was elected to the position. Many politicians in the state of New York were unhappy to see the Rough Rider gain control of the state's most powerful political position. Among those who opposed Roosevelt was Thomas C. "Boss" Platt. Platt was a state senator and a very powerful political figure in New York. His supporters were powerful businessmen who, under Platt's agenda, could continue to control large markets and ignore the needs of their workers. Platt knew immediately that Roosevelt would cause him problems.

Roosevelt didn't like Boss Platt any more than Platt liked him. He believed that Platt was just the kind of elected official that should be removed from office. But Roosevelt also knew he could not afford to wage an open war on Platt, who was an elected official in his own party. Instead, Roosevelt kept his opinion about Boss Platt to himself and instead started pushing bills through that gave workers more rights and reorganized tax laws that favored the wealthy. This made Platt furious.

Meanwhile, at home, Roosevelt enjoyed spending time with his growing family. After they moved into the governor's mansion, Edith immediately began redecorating and spent most of her time replacing the mansion's drab, run-down furniture with newer pieces. The governor spent a great deal of his time playing with his children, chasing them around the house and reading them stories from books. He also taught the children about the outdoors and taught them to appreciate the wild plants and animals that lived in the forests surrounding the mansion. Roosevelt's children also shared his love of animals, and visitors to the home had to be on the lookout for the pet hamsters, guinea pigs, and rabbits that ran free throughout the lower floors of the mansion.

Boss Platt realized that he could not ruin Roosevelt's reputation. People in New York and across the country were fascinated by Roosevelt's rough-and-tumble personality and large crowds gathered whenever he gave public speeches. Meanwhile, Roosevelt had aspirations to be more than a governor. Instead, he wanted to be named as secretary of war, but lost his chance when President McKinley nominated Elihu Root instead. Roosevelt's friend Henry Cabot Lodge asked him to run as McKinley's vice president. Roosevelt replied that he wasn't interested.

It seemed, though, that Roosevelt was going to have very little say in the matter. His popularity had drawn the attention of the entire Republican Party, and they knew if Roosevelt appeared as McKinley's running mate, the Republican Party was all but guaranteed to win the 1900 presidential election. Roosevelt, however, saw the office of vice president as a weak position that had very little say regarding political matters. In addition, he believed that vice presidents were rarely nominated by the party to later run for president. When Roosevelt was considering running, it had been 60 years since a vice president was last elected president.

However, Roosevelt was finding it hard to say no. It seemed the whole Republican Party, and most of the country, was counting on him to be vice president. His strongest supporter, oddly enough, was his enemy Boss Platt. Platt knew very well that if Roosevelt became vice president, he would be away from New York politics and Platt would regain the power he had lost during Roosevelt's watch.

President William McKinley and Vice President Theodore Roosevelt stand on a porch step circa 1900.

Roosevelt attended the Republican Convention in 1900 and found that there were already buttons being made that said "McKinley-Roosevelt 1900." Crowds chanted "We want Teddy! We want Teddy!" whenever Roosevelt gave speeches. The scene was set. McKinley asked Roosevelt to be his running mate in 1900. Roosevelt could not refuse the offer and the 1900 election was a Republican landslide.

McKinley was a stern and dour man, which appealed to many of the older members of the party. Roosevelt was a firecracker who seemed about to explode at any moment. He gave passionate speeches that excited the American public.

Despite this apparent good news, Edith Roosevelt had only just finished decorating the New York Governor's Mansion when she and the children was forced to move to Washington. Roosevelt was also depressed. He felt that by becoming vice president, he had no future in politics and called his new position "the fifth wheel to the coach."

As it turned out, Roosevelt would not be vice president for very long. While on a speaking engagement with the Vermont Fish and Game League about conservation issues, President McKinley attended the 1900 Pan-American Expo in Buffalo, New York. Nowadays, all presidential appearances are closely guarded, but back then, it was not the case. President McKinley spent hours shaking hands at the expo, listening to the concerns of the American people. The last hand he shook was that of Leon Czolgosz, an anarchist who wanted to assassinate the President. As they shook hands, Czolgosz pulled a revolver from his coat and shot McKinley in the chest. (Czolgosz was arrested and later executed.)

Roosevelt rushed to Washington when he heard the news about the shooting. He found that the president was doing better than expected. In fact, at first it appeared that McKinley would make a full recovery as the assassin's bullet had not hit any major organs.

Roosevelt decided his family needed a break from the fast pace of life in the capital and so he gathered his family and headed to the Adirondacks. His life had changed drastically over the past year and, as always, Roosevelt needed to spend time in the wilderness to escape the pressures of political life and reconnect with nature.

Yet the most dramatic change in Roosevelt's life was yet to come. While he and his family were climbing Mount Moray in the Adirondacks, President McKinley's condition suddenly worsened and he died unexpectedly. No one was able to contact Vice President Roosevelt for some time until a messenger climbed partway up Mount Moray and found him.

Roosevelt immediately headed back to Washington, D.C. He was to be sworn in as president of the United States.

The Presidency

The worst nightmare of the New York politician Boss Platt had come true. The pugnacious governor Theodore Roosevelt, who Platt was sure had lost all his political power when he became vice president, had become the most powerful man in America. Roosevelt took office on September 23, 1901, the day his father would have turned 70 years old. Roosevelt thought this to be a good sign. When Roosevelt became president, life for the White House staff changed completely. Having the Roosevelts in the White House was very different than having President McKinley there. Roosevelt and his wife had six children (seven, some joked, when you counted the president). The White House became very much like Roosevelt's boyhood home. Staff members and visitors had to be on lookout for pet snakes, rats, rabbits, and birds. Quentin, Archie, and their friends called themselves the "White House Gang" and continually pestered guests and staff by running through the house, screaming and romping with their pets. Roosevelt's daughter Alice, for example, carried a green snake she named Emily Spinach in her

New president Theodore Roosevelt takes the oath of office in Buffalo, New York, at the home of Ansley Wilcox and wife Mary Grace Rumsey in 1901.

purse. The White House was also home to a badger named Josiah, Bill the lizard, Nibble the mouse, and a parrot named Loretta that said, "Hurrah for Roosevelt," among other pets. Once when Archie was sick and in bed, Quentin brought their pony up in the White House elevator to cheer him up.

President Roosevelt enjoyed being with his children and did his best to give all of them his attention. He was often seen running through the White House, chasing them up and down stairs and playing hide-and-seek with them. If Roosevelt made an appointment to play with his children, he would keep it, even halting meetings so as not to disappoint them.

ROOSEVELT TAKES CHARGE

As much as Roosevelt enjoyed his children, he still had the nation's business to deal with. One of the first issues he faced was a dispute between coal workers and coal mine owners. Roosevelt had always been opposed to greedy industrialists having so much power in America and believed that someday the working class would rise up in what he called a "riotous, wicked day of atonement." Coal miners protested that they had to work in very poor conditions for little money. The coal mine owners, meanwhile, were some of the wealthiest men in America and were out to make as much money as they could, regardless of the consequences for the miners.

In the spring of 1902, the miners finally became fed up with the treatment they had been receiving at the hand of wealthy mine owners and went on strike. The impact of the strike was immediate and severe. By the first part of the twentieth century, many homes and businesses were heated by coal furnaces and trains were powered by coal to carry goods across the country. With no coal being mined because of the strike, the country faced a disaster. When winter came, families who lived in the coldest parts of the country would not have had coal to heat their homes, a situation that could have resulted in riots and violence.

Roosevelt knew he had to act quickly. The coal miners refused to give in to the miner's demands. The miners, on the other hand, flatly refused to return to work without being given more rights and better wages. Coal miners at that time earned very little money and oftentimes suffered from diseases that were caused by breathing coal dust. They worked long hours, seven days a week.

When Roosevelt realized the mine owners were going to refuse to accept any demands from the miners' union, he stepped in and threatened to use military force to take over the mines to protect the millions of Americans who would be affected by the coal shortage. The mine owners backed down, and coal miners won a pay increase and a nine-hour work day.

Roosevelt had always distrusted powerful businessmen and, at that time, no businessman in America was as powerful as J.P. Morgan, a railroad owner whose large fortune was worth more than all of the gold and silver in the United States. Morgan controlled almost all of the goods going into and coming out of the Northwest. Roosevelt did not believe that one man had the right to have so

Theodore and Edith Roosevelt pose with their six children (*left to right*): Quentin, Theodore Jr., Archie, Alice, Kermit, and Ethel.

much control over the railroad industry and claimed that Morgan's Northern Securities, the company that owned and operated all of the railroad companies in the northwestern United States, was a monopoly. He set out to break up this powerful company.

Morgan was furious, but Roosevelt carried on with his "trust busting" campaign to break up single companies that dominated a single industry. Many Republicans disagreed with the president's policies, since they received political support from large businesses like Northern Securities. But the majority of Americans stood firmly beside the president and applauded his efforts to break up these large trusts. His fiery speeches were attended by thousands of people and his "bully pulpit," as he called it, was a perfect platform for Roosevelt to address the public about issues that he felt were very important.

Another issue that troubled Roosevelt was how food was handled by food companies. Meat packers, for example, routinely processed sick and dying cattle and sometimes even butchered cattle that were already dead. Rats were ground up and packaged along with the meat. Appalled at the way food was handled by workers, Roosevelt signed two very important pieces of legislation into law: the Pure Food and Drug Act and the Meat Inspection Act. These laws required food and drug companies to obey regulations and gave the government the power to inspect meatpacking facilities.

Roosevelt's interests went beyond domestic problems. He was very aware of issues that involved other countries, and he believed that the United States had an important role in international affairs. Among his achievements in international affairs was the digging of a canal through Central America that would allow ships to cross from the Atlantic to the Pacific—the Panama Canal.

Back then, American ships on the East Coast of the United States had to travel all around the southernmost tip of South America to reach the West Coast. Many believed that there should be a canal built that would allow more direct access from the Atlantic Ocean to the Pacific Ocean, but there was disagreement on whether it should be built through Panama or Nicaragua. At that time, Panama was controlled by Columbia, and although Roosevelt believed it made sense to build a canal across Panama, he had no intention of paying the $40 million that Columbia demanded before they would allow the United States to build it.

Meanwhile, Panama had been threatening a revolution against Columbia for some time. President Roosevelt realized that if Panama became independent from Columbia, it would be much simpler and cheaper to build a canal across Panama. Although Roosevelt denied backing the Panamanian Revolution, he was certainly aware that a revolution was coming and did nothing to stop it.

Columbia had a very small military occupation force in Panama at the time, and so when the Panamanian Revolution began in November 1903, it was over in less than two days. The United States soon began construction on the Panama Canal in the spring of 1904. When it was complete, the canal would reduce the distance that a ship had to travel from New York to reach San Francisco from 14,000 miles (22,530.8 km) to only 6,000 (9,656 km). The canal would be almost 50 miles (80.4 km) long, and the water would be controlled by a series of locks. The construction of the canal was very hard and dangerous work. Many members of the canal's construction crew were killed by injuries or caught yellow fever, a disease spread by mosquitoes. Yet when it was complete, it was clear that the Panama Canal was one of the greatest feats of human engineering ever attempted. President Roosevelt traveled to Panama in 1906 to witness the construction of the canal firsthand and became the first president to ever travel outside the United States while in office.

Roosevelt was well known for his strong personality and sometimes aggressive nature. Even though Roosevelt had earned a Medal of Honor for his part in the war with Spain over Cuba, a war which he himself worked very hard to start, Roosevelt earned a Nobel Peace Prize for his part in stopping another war. Across the Pacific Ocean, Russia and Japan were both very strong nations and conflict between them seemed inevitable. Despite many difficulties, Roosevelt managed to get the leaders of both countries to meet in New Hampshire to discuss their differences. Roosevelt tried his best to stay out of the direct negotiations between the Japanese and Russian leaders and remain in the role of a mediator. Nevertheless, it appeared that even Roosevelt's best efforts to avoid a war had failed, and as the meeting drew to a close, he returned to Oyster Bay. However, much to his surprise, both sides reached an agreement just before the meeting ended. Roosevelt's part in stopping the Russo-Japanese War earned him the 1906 Nobel Peace Prize.

Alton B. Parker was the Democratic Party's presidential candidate nominated to run against Roosevelt in the 1904 election. Parker was a judge from Roosevelt's home state of New York, and although Parker was well liked by many, he could not match Roosevelt's passionate style, which had earned him so many fans across the country. After a campaign tour that took him across the country, Roosevelt won the 1904 election by a landslide. Roosevelt was thrilled by his win but, just after this victory, he made a mistake that he would regret for the rest of his life. He agreed that his second term in office would be his last; he would not run for reelection.

THE PRESIDENT AS CONSERVATIONIST

Roosevelt accomplished many things as president, but his most important achievements were the conservation initiatives he signed into law. The Industrial Revolution had made the United States a wealthy country, but an attitude had developed among many Americans that the best way for the United States to continue increasing its wealth was to utilize the country's resources at any cost. Railroad companies cut through the western United States while loggers cut down huge stands of forest as quickly as possible. Game animals had once been abundant on the plains and in the foothills of the Rocky Mountains, but unregulated hunting and trapping had caused a huge decline in the number of animals. Bison herds, which once numbered in the millions, had been killed off until only a handful remained in Yellowstone National Park. Even in Yellowstone, the bison were illegally hunted by poachers, and it appeared that it would not be long before the species was gone forever.

Roosevelt was among the first people to publicize the damage that westerners were doing to the plains and the animals that lived there. While he was a rancher in the Dakota Territory, much of the game was killed off or driven out to make room for cattle. Roosevelt had started pushing for conservation reform when he was president of the Boone and Crockett Club many years before. Now he was starting to see the benefits of the efforts he and others had made on behalf of wild animals. In 1903, he went on a cross-country tour and arrived at Yellowstone National Park to find it teeming with game. He spent one whole afternoon trying to count all of the elk in a

With a railroad car behind him, President Roosevelt enters Yellowstone Park in 1902 on horseback.

single Yellowstone herd and finally gave up when his count reached an estimate of about 3,000 animals in the herd.

Before Roosevelt took office, there were four national parks—Yellowstone, Yosemite's High Country, and two groves of redwood trees in California called General Grant and Sequoia. These parks covered a relatively small percentage of the country, and even they were not fully protected. Yellowstone was becoming commercialized as tourists came to stay in the park's hotels and rode on stagecoaches across the landscape. They often littered the park with glass bottles or carved their names into the delicate mineral walls of the geysers. The U.S. Cavalry was placed in charge of maintaining the parks, but even they could do very little to control this abuse. Roosevelt took note of this damage and made plans to put a stop to it.

After leaving Yellowstone, Roosevelt headed south to the Grand Canyon in Arizona. He looked down into the massive canyon walls

A wagon carrying President Roosevelt, with John Muir sitting behind him, stops in front of a redwood tree in California circa 1903.

that had been eroded over millions of years to see the thin line of sparkling water that was the Colorado River. He marveled at the colors of the rocks that made up the canyon—streaks of magenta and deep rusty red woven into sheets of orange and deep brown. The sheer size of the canyon was amazing. During this trip, Roosevelt told one crowd of listeners of the wonders of the canyon and concluded that they should, "Leave it as it is. You cannot improve it."

The next stop on Roosevelt's 1903 tour was California. There he met up with the well-known naturalist John Muir. A nature lover like Roosevelt, Muir was a thin man with a long gray beard and was a passionate expert on the plants and animals of northern California. Muir's favorite place was Yosemite National Park. When Roosevelt came to Yosemite, he asked Muir to be his personal guide. Roosevelt was amazed by the natural beauty he found in Yosemite, by the towering waterfalls and great evergreen forests that lined the mountainsides, and by the lush valleys that nestled between the craggy peaks of the Sierra Nevada Mountains. Muir asked Roosevelt to create laws that would control what could and what could not be done in America's national parks and to limit the logging and overhunting that threatened to wipe out the ecosystem that Muir loved so much.

March 1903. At that time, it was very fashionable for women in New York to wear hats that were adorned with bird feathers. Many of these feathers were taken from wetland birds that inhabited Florida; for example, egrets that were shot while they were sitting in their nests. One ornithologist (scientist who studies birds) estimated that he saw feathers belonging to forty different bird species on ladies' hats in New York City.

Pelican Island on Florida's east coast was one of the major sources of bird feathers. "Plume hunters," as they were called, would travel in their boats along the waterways near the mouth of the Indian River at Pelican Island and shoot any birds they found nesting. This was an easy and profitable way for them to make money because the feathers were worth more per pound than gold.

Theodore Roosevelt stands with John Muir on Glacier Point in Yosemite Valley in California circa 1906.

The answer to the Pelican Island dilemma was much simpler than Roosevelt could have imagined. He asked one of his officials what laws there were that said he could not declare a bird refuge. The official answered there were none, so Roosevelt shouted, "Very well. I declare it!" With that statement, Pelican Island became the first of many refuges that Roosevelt made by a simple declaration. This immediately put a stop to the unlawful killing of the birds of Pelican Island.

Roosevelt began placing more land under federal control. As John Muir had asked, he expanded the boundaries of Yosemite National Park and placed the park under federal protection so that corrupt officials in California could not access the park's resources for their own profit. Muir was thrilled. The land he had so enjoyed showing to the president of the United States was now safe.

While on another 1903 trip into the wilderness, Roosevelt created a toy sensation that has lasted over one hundred years. While hunting in the swamps of Louisiana, he came upon a small bear that had been captured and tied to a tree so that he could shoot it. Roosevelt was furious and demanded that the bear be set free, saying he would not shoot an animal tied to a tree because it was neither fair nor sporting. His refusal to kill the bear soon became news. As a result, a toy maker in New York created a stuffed bear in Roosevelt's honor and called it the "teddy bear."

Throughout the rest of his presidency, Roosevelt did his best to claim wilderness areas for public use and to control the utilization of the country's natural resources. John F. Lacey, a congressman from Iowa, helped Roosevelt greatly by pushing legislation through that would allow for the preservation of "antiquities," defined as items of historical value. Lacey was outraged by the theft of artifacts from ancient Indian sites, which would then be sold to museums at a profit. The main area of concern was the Chaco Canyon region of New Mexico, where Native American artifacts were being taken and sold so fast that Lacey feared archeologists would never be able to examine the ruins. This law was officially called An Act for the Preservation of American Antiquities. It allowed the president the power to declare areas as national monuments and was later called the Antiquities Act. The Antiquities Act of 1906 gave presidents the power to proclaim any area a national monument.

The first national monument declared by Theodore Roosevelt was Devil's Tower, a giant shaft of igneous rock that rises above the plains of northeastern Wyoming. Roosevelt named several national monuments during his presidency, including Chaco

This stuffed bear, called "Teddy," was presented to Kermit Roosevelt by the Ideal Toy Company in 1903. This "teddy bear" was among the first to be produced.

Canyon National Monument, making it illegal to take artifacts from these historic sites or damage them in any way.

However, there were still some questions about how to enforce laws in national parks. Even though Roosevelt set aside millions of

PELICAN ISLAND

Theodore Roosevelt's first conservation initiative as president was to declare Pelican Island, Florida, a federal bird reserve in March 1903. Today, Pelican Island is a national wildlife refuge. Each year, visitors come to Pelican Island to view and photograph the wide variety of water birds that build their nests and raise their chicks on the island. Even though Pelican Island was declared what was called a bird reserve, the water birds that nested there still faced serious risks.

Fifteen years after Roosevelt declared Pelican Island a reserve, fishermen in the area protested that the pelicans living on the island were competing with them for the large number of fish that they depended on for their livelihood. These fishermen began killing the island's pelican chicks, but enforcement of wildlife laws helped put a stop to the killing. Later, Pelican Island's bird populations faced yet another threat when developers attempted to build on the island. A group of concerned citizens formed a coalition called the Indian River Area Preservation League. Plans for development were stopped, and Pelican Island became a national historic landmark in 1963, further protecting it from exploitation. In 1993, Pelican Island was named as a Wetland of International Importance by members of the Ramsar Convention, which identifies wetlands of international importance and works to insure they are properly preserved. Today, visitors to Pelican Island enjoy its pristine habitat and large numbers of nesting water birds.

acres for public use, there were still very few laws outlining what could and what could not be done in national parks and forests. Adding to this problem was the fact that there was no clear understanding of who would enforce laws within park boundaries. The U.S. Cavalry had this responsibility before, but because they were military soldiers, they had no right to arrest anyone. In 1905, Roosevelt developed a plan to form a government body that would be charged with maintaining many of the areas he had placed under the U.S. government's responsibility. He called this organization the National Forest Service and named Gifford Pinchot as its head in 1905.

Pinchot was a tall, thin man with wide, brown eyes and a large black moustache that drooped over his mouth. He had been trained in Germany and considered himself the first truly qualified forester in the United States. Unlike Roosevelt's friend John Muir, who believed that the government should set aside parks and leave them completely alone, Pinchot thought that the best way to protect forests was to leave them open to the public and limit the activities that took place within them. Pinchot believed that forests could be logged, cut down, and even burned, and that they would remain healthy if their use was carefully managed and controlled by trained professionals in the National Forest Service. Pinchot's belief that trained Forest Service employees could effectively manage America's forests proved to be correct.

Roosevelt had accomplished more toward protecting America's natural resources in seven years in office than had been done since American independence in 1776. He placed more than 200 million acres (80,937,128 hectares) under the protection of the United States government and preserved the land by writing laws regarding the acceptable use of resources within protected areas. More importantly, Roosevelt understood that America's wilderness was something that every American had the right to enjoy, regardless of race, religious belief, or social class.

When the 1908 election neared, Roosevelt made good on his word and agreed that he would not run for a third term. He supported his good friend William Howard Taft for the presidency.

CAREERS IN CONSERVATION

You don't have to be the president of the United States to get involved in protecting wild places. There are a variety of career options for people who enjoy being outdoors and helping preserve and protect wildlife. One possible career option is wildlife law enforcement. This career involves upholding the laws that govern the use of public lands and the harvest of wildlife. New advancement in forensics has allowed wildlife law enforcement personnel to employ the same tactics used on human crime scenes to determine who killed animals that have been taken illegally. The United States Forest Service also hires people to work as range management specialists. Range management specialists study ecosystems and try to prevent problems like the overgrazing that Theodore Roosevelt saw during his ranching days in the Dakota Territory.

The Forest Service's work is not limited to grasslands, though. Range management specialists work in a variety of habitats to be sure that the ecosystem is not in danger. To do this, range management specialists oversee grazing by livestock herds on public land and determine a maximum capacity of livestock that the ecosystem can support. This greatly reduces the chances that public lands will be overgrazed. Range managers also conduct soil tests, examine the effects of erosion, and develop programs to reduce the spread of invasive species.

Taft, a judge from Cincinnati, Ohio, had served as Roosevelt's secretary of war and really wanted to be named chief justice of the Supreme Court instead of president. Taft was a huge man with a curl-tipped moustache. Despite Taft's misgivings about being president, his wife, Nellie, pushed him into accepting the nomination.

Roosevelt threw his support behind Taft and watched as he soundly beat William Jennings Bryan at the polls in November 1908.

Roosevelt's term as president had ended. His term in office had been a resounding success: He had brought about improvements for workers, better food sanitation, and had protected much of America's wilderness. Even after all these accomplishments, Roosevelt still had not lost his love of exploration. After leaving the White House, he planned what he called "my last chance at something in the nature of a great adventure."

8

Journey into Africa and Out of the White House

On April 21, 1909, Theodore Roosevelt set his eyes on a goal he had dreamed of since his childhood. For a man who had been a war hero, a western cowboy, and the most powerful man in America, this was a dream come true. After the ship on which he was sailing docked at the port of Mombasa, British East Africa, Roosevelt stepped down and looked around at the bustling port city, which was being pounded by steady rain. Roosevelt was in Africa once again—this time as an adult.

Since his childhood, Roosevelt had read about the adventures of intrepid explorers who traveled across the African continent in search of game and wealth. Now, Roosevelt himself would set out in search of the one thing he loved most—a wilderness adventure.

Kermit accompanied his father on the expedition, which was funded largely by private donations and the $50,000 dollars *Scribner's* had agreed to pay Roosevelt for his articles about hunting Africa's wild game. The expedition had a scientific basis as well, as it was accompanied by scientists and taxidermists. The scientists were along to take careful measurements of each animal Roosevelt killed and record them in journals, while the taxidermists were there to be in charge of seeing that the animals' skins were preserved and sent back to the Smithsonian Institute for further study and cataloging. For Roosevelt, a boy who cataloged and recorded the measurements of frogs and mice he caught as a boy in New York, hunting in Africa was the ultimate thrill.

From Mombasa, Roosevelt and his party set out via train for the Kapati Plains where his safari would truly begin. Joining him on the expedition was British naturalist, explorer, and soldier Frederic Courtney Selous. Selous' previous writings about his travels across

Former President Roosevelt and Baron Rudolf V. Stalin Pacha ride camels in the Khartoum Desert around 1909. The ride was part of Roosevelt's year-long safari after leaving office.

the African continent had inspired Roosevelt, and now the former president had the thrill of being in the very same continent with his hero Selous.

During the trip across the Kapati plains, Roosevelt sat on a seat built across the front of the train just above the cattle catcher (a steel skirt shaped like a plow that was designed to push obstacles out of the train's path). Roosevelt thoroughly enjoyed watching the birds and mammals of the plains as they ran away from the oncoming train. As an amateur ornithologist, Roosevelt was thrilled by the variety of bird species he saw. There were large, olive-colored bustards that stalked through the grass in search of insects. Tiny bee-eaters, brilliantly colored birds that ate flying insects, swarmed about the rushing train. A hornbill, a large black and white bird with a large curved bill, flew up from the tracks, so close to the train that Roosevelt nearly caught it.

The birds of Africa were very interesting to Roosevelt, but it was wild game that interested him most of all. The plains of British East Africa were filled with a wide variety of game. Brown, shaggy waterbuck watched the train pass from the cover of tall grass. Herds of zebra rushed across the tracks, a long stream of flashing black and white animals that passed just before the train reached them. Herds of delicate impala and sturdy hartebeest galloped in every direction in front of Roosevelt. He could not have been more excited.

On the Kapati Plains, Roosevelt met up with the rest of his party. This year-long safari was a massive operation that employed over 250 native porters who followed behind the former president as they carried tents, ammunition, taxidermy supplies, and clothing. The scientists accompanying Roosevelt brought four tons (3.6 metric tons) of salt with them to dry the skins for shipment back to the United States, all of which had to be carried by the porters. Roosevelt himself brought along almost 40 hardcover books and read whenever he had the chance.

Having long been a man who prided himself on taking risks, Roosevelt eagerly awaited his chance to hunt Africa's "big five," the most dangerous animals in Africa, according to professional hunters

AFRICA'S DOG DAYS

Roosevelt saw more open land and wild game in Africa than he could have imagined. Today, however, the increasing human population on the African continent oftentimes reduces the amount of land available for wild animals. As humans and animals come into contact more and more often, problems arise. This is particularly true when large predators like lions, hyenas, and cheetahs feed on a farmer's livestock. In many parts of Africa, wild predators that kill livestock are shot on sight.

Dr. Laurie Marker of the Cheetah Conservation Fund in Namibia has developed an ingenious way to keep farmers from killing cheetahs that prey on livestock. This method involves introducing Anatolian shepherd dogs into the herds of goats and sheep. Anatolian shepherds originated in Turkey where they were used to defend flocks of sheep against wolves and other large predators. In Namibia, these dogs are raised for the same purpose. By providing farmers with Anatolian puppies that are trained to keep the cheetahs away, many fewer goats and sheep are lost and, in turn, the farmers do not have to kill the cheetahs. Dr. Marker's ingenious idea gives new meaning to the phrase "fighting like cats and dogs."

and explorers at that time. The big five included the massive but nearly blind rhinoceros, the elephant, the surly cape buffalo, the lion, and the leopard. Of them all, Roosevelt most wanted to hunt a lion and soon got his wish. Shortly after arriving at the Kapati Plains, Roosevelt took his first, a large male. It was an accomplishment that led to much celebration. Before the safari had ended Roosevelt killed eight more lions.

One of Roosevelt's most harrowing encounters was with a rhinoceros. The rhino bull was startled when Roosevelt and his group stumbled upon it, and it charged them at full speed. Roosevelt was very calm as took aim with his rifle and fired, dropping it at close range. Had Roosevelt missed, the rhino would almost surely have killed one or more members of the party. Roosevelt was very pleased with the whole ordeal and posed proudly beside the fallen rhino. After this, the native trackers began to have faith in the round man with the spectacles and wide smile. They nicknamed Roosevelt *Bwana Mkuba,* or "Big Chief." It was a nickname that Roosevelt thoroughly enjoyed having.

Theodore Roosevelt stands behind a dead rhino, which was later mounted for museum use, during his African safari circa 1909.

The goal of Roosevelt's trip was not to simply kill animals. He was also there to take specimens for the Smithsonian—gathering representative samples of each species, which usually meant a male, a female, and one of their young. The taxidermists worked feverishly to keep up with Roosevelt's hunting. Whenever an animal was killed, there was a lot that needed to be done in a short period of time: the skin removed and preserved; the meat prepared to provide food for the staff; and, lastly, the bones would have to be cleaned and preserved.

Roosevelt was a conservationist at heart and truly believed that hunting was an essential part of effective wildlife management. It helped raise funds for further conservation, feed the hungry, and control wildlife populations. Roosevelt believed that "to protest against all hunting of game is a sign of softness of head, not of soundness of heart."

At the end of 11 months, Roosevelt had collected a large number of animals including 17 lions, 20 rhinoceroses, 11 elephants, and 9 giraffes. Roosevelt also managed to collect samples of very elusive animals like the bongo, a red-orange antelope with large ears and spiraling, white-tipped horns that lives in the dense forests of central Africa. Both Roosevelt and Kermit were in perfect health after their trip through the African wilderness. When the safari ended in Khartoum, the capital of Sudan, the Roosevelt party had collected 512 animals.

ONE MORE RUN FOR OFFICE

After Roosevelt's African safari had ended, he met up with Edith and they traveled together to Europe where Roosevelt was greeted with much fanfare as crowds gathered in England and Italy to see the Rough Rider and former president they had read so much about. Roosevelt did not disappoint. He was happy to give speeches and flash his toothy smile at every opportunity.

Yet Roosevelt was not at all happy about the reports he was receiving from the United States. Gifford Pinchot, Roosevelt's choice as the leader of the newly created Forest Service, had gotten into an argument with Taft regarding coal mine development in Alaska that ended with Taft deciding to fire Pinchot. This news infuriated Roosevelt. Taft and Roosevelt's old friendship was under a great deal of strain when Roosevelt returned from Europe. Taft had been Roosevelt's choice for president, but now Roosevelt was forced to rethink that decision. As the two men disagreed more and more often, the tension between them reached a boiling point. Roosevelt

PROTECTING THE AMAZON

When Theodore Roosevelt explored the River of Doubt, much of the Amazon rainforest was unexplored. Even today much of the area around the River of Doubt is uninhabited and remote. The Amazon rainforest covers almost one and a half billion acres in nine South American countries. Scientists have found tens of thousands different species of plants in the Amazon, and more are being discovered every year, many of which are very important to medicine. Some of these plants may provide cures for serious illnesses. A variety of rare and endangered species also live in this rainforest, including jaguars, marmosets, tapirs, anteaters, sloths, and a wide variety of birds.

Yet the Amazon now faces the threat of deforestation—the cutting down and clearing away of the forest's trees for profit. Most of the trees have been removed so that farmers would have more acreage to graze cattle on. There have also been tests recently that show that the health of the rainforest is very closely related to the overall health of the environment worldwide. Several agencies, including the World Wildlife Fund, are cooperating to reduce the rate of rainforest loss in the Amazon.

began calling Taft a "fathead." In turn, Taft called Roosevelt "a man who can't tell the truth."

Roosevelt finally concluded that Taft was an incompetent president and decided to run for the White House again in 1912, this time as a member of the newly formed Progressive or "Bull Moose" Party. He campaigned fiercely and gained many supporters for his newly formed party. He was so intensely committed that after he was shot by a man named John Schrank during a campaign speech in Milwaukee on October 14, 1912, he immediately went on to deliver a portion of the 50-page speech he had prepared for the evening before going to the hospital.

Roosevelt survived the shooting, but lost the 1912 presidential election to Woodrow Wilson. Taft finished a distant third behind Wilson and Roosevelt. It meant the end of both Roosevelt's new "Bull Moose" Party and his political career. As he had often done in times of trial, Roosevelt escaped to the wilderness following his loss. This time he headed for the unexplored Amazon rainforest to accompany scientists as they traveled down the unmapped River of Doubt in Brazil. Roosevelt called the trip "my last chance to be a boy." Roosevelt's son Kermit also accompanied him on this trip.

ROOSEVELT'S FINAL—AND MOST DANGEROUS—ADVENTURE

In the spring of 1913, Roosevelt was asked to give a series of lectures across South America. Following these speeches, Roosevelt, Kermit, and a group of scientists from the American Museum of Natural History set out to explore the River of Doubt and collect specimens. The headwaters of the river are located in the western Brazilian province of Rondonia near the border with Bolivia, and this river flows for four hundred miles through the jungle before emptying into the Amazon River. The River of Doubt earned its name because even local fishermen would not explore the middle portion of the river because of the violent rapids and large waterfalls that made travel extremely dangerous. Roosevelt's expedition set out from the headwaters in seven wooden canoes with enough rations for 50 days.

Roosevelt immensely enjoyed his time observing the brilliant birds and exotic mammals that inhabited the thick, green rainforests of the Amazon. But it wasn't long before the group ran into hardships. The River of Doubt had many difficult rapids along its course, for which the wooden boats were unsuitable. Each perilous trip through a violently churning rapid could mean death for any of the men aboard and, indeed, it wasn't long before the group suffered their first loss when one of the men fell overboard, never to be seen again.

While on his Brazilian expedition in 1913, Theodore Roosevelt (*second from left*) helped hold up a jaguar skin that would be shipped home for mounting.

Indeed, the River of Doubt proved more challenging than even Roosevelt had imagined. In some places, the river was too shallow to allow for passage of the heavy wooden boats, so the men had to carry the boats over land through the thick jungle before they could return to the river to continue the voyage. It was hard work, especially for a man of Roosevelt's age. There seemed to be no end to the fierce rapids: As soon as one rapid was forded, another was sure to follow. The wooden boats were not up to the task and became battered and lost in the churning water. When the group had finally lost all but two of their boats, they had to stop and build more before continuing.

Furthermore, none of them knew what tribes lived along the river and how these people would react when they were approached by strangers. In addition, several varieties of venomous snakes lived along the river's edge and each day was an agonizing fight against hordes of swarming, biting insects such as fire ants and mosquitoes. One of the crew members went mad, stole a large portion of the group's food, shot one of the expedition leaders, and ran off into the rainforest never to be heard from again.

Roosevelt himself suffered greatly on the trip. While he was trying to save one of the boats in the rapids, he seriously injured his leg. Soon after, the leg became infected, swelling and turning red. Roosevelt ran a fever of 105° Fahrenheit (40.5° Celsius) and asked that his men leave him behind to die. He also came down with dysentery, a digestive disorder that results from drinking contaminated water, and malaria. Roosevelt's condition became frightful. As he suffered from incredible pain in his infected leg and the agony of dysentery and malaria, he started to recite the same line of poetry over and over. For a time, he even considered suicide.

Finally, on the forty-eighth day of their journey, the group reached a village at the end of the river where a boat was brought to them. Roosevelt survived, though he had lost a great deal of weight and was very frail for some time. In his honor, the local people changed the name of the river to Rio Teodoro: "Theodore's River."

The former president returned to Sagamore Hill to recuperate. His time in the Amazon had been a great adventure for Roosevelt but the trip had taken a toll on him. Even though he hoped to avoid any talk of politics, it seemed that Roosevelt would never be able to avoid the subject as long as he lived.

Roosevelt was again a national hero. There was some talk of his running again as a Progressive Party candidate for president in 1916. Woodrow Wilson had almost finished his first term and was preparing to run for reelection against the Republican nominee. Roosevelt hoped secretly that he would get the Republican nomination, but this was not the case. The Republicans nominated Charles Evans Hughes instead. Roosevelt's chances of ever becoming president again were very slim, and Wilson won reelection.

In 1915, a British ship called the *Lusitania* traveling off the coast of Europe sank after being fired upon by a German submarine. Almost 2,000 people were killed, including more than 100 Americans. To Roosevelt, this was an act of war and he thought the United States should join the Allied Forces and begin an attack on Germany immediately. He was furious when Woodrow Wilson refused to go to war and raged that America was "passing through a thick streak of yellow in our national life." Eventually, though, the United States decided to enter World War I and, on April 2, 1917 officially declared war on Germany. Roosevelt desperately wanted to lead another division of volunteer soldiers, just as he had against the Spanish in Cuba. However, President Wilson was having none of it. Nevertheless, many members of Roosevelt's family fought in the First World War. Archie, Ted, and Quentin fought for the United States and Kermit, who had accompanied his father on so many adventures, chose to fight with the British forces. Roosevelt managed to join the fight himself in a way as he traveled around the country giving speeches to promote the war effort.

Roosevelt had been through a lot in his life: He fought in a war, survived the loss of his beloved wife and mother on the same night, and had endured tremendous hardships while exploring the Amazon. Nothing, however, could prepare him for the shock and agony that beset him in July 1918 when a dispatch delivered to Sagamore

Hill informed him that his youngest son Quentin, a fighter pilot, had been shot down and killed behind enemy lines. Roosevelt was stunned. The war he had fought so hard to wage had now taken the life of his youngest son.

After Quentin's death, Roosevelt kept himself busy writing letters to friends while also writing a column for the *Kansas City Star*. He remained determined to keep his hand in politics and his letters to his friends often tried to persuade them to his point of view. Yet he was suffering both physically and emotionally. Still crushed by the loss of Quentin, Roosevelt also battled with gout and rheumatism. Near the end of his life, he had trouble breathing and was almost always in pain.

Just after midnight on January 6, 1919, Theodore Roosevelt died at the home he loved so much, the home he had built on Sagamore Hill, the same hill where he stood as a boy and shouted poetry into the wind. He was 60 years old. Archie informed his brothers of their father's passing in a brief but powerful message: "The old lion is dead."

Roosevelt's Legacy

Today, no cattle graze in the pastures and valleys where Theodore Roosevelt's Elkhorn Ranch once stood. All of the cowboys that once drove herds across the prairie along the banks of the Little Missouri are gone.

Yet the plains are not empty. In the springtime, a new rush of thick, green grass rises from the prairie. The great herds of cattle that once decimated the prairie grass have been replaced by deer, elk, and pronghorn antelope. Prairie dogs build intricate tunnels beneath the earth and sit aboveground on their haunches watching out for predators. In the evening, coyotes howl from the top of the multi-colored pillars of rock that give the Badlands their name. Large, round hoofprints can be found along the river and out into the plains. Even the bison have returned.

Roosevelt was the first to raise alarm about the damage that was being done to the environment of the Great Plains. Even though he was a rancher, he knew that the ranchers' desire for large profits would destroy the wild beauty of the prairie and worked to stop the destruction. Nearly 100 years later, in 1978, Theodore Roosevelt National Park was established in North Dakota in honor of the former president. Roosevelt's own ranches became part of the national park, protecting the prairie forever.

Throughout his life, Roosevelt was fascinated by the natural world. During his youth, he wanted to be a naturalist and write papers about wild animals so that he would have an impact on science. Yet Roosevelt's accomplishments as president went much

Theodore Roosevelt National Park in North Dakota sits on 110 square miles (285 square kilometers) of land. The entire park is surrounded by a 7-foot-tall (2.1-meters-tall) stretch of woven wire fencing that keeps bison and feral horses inside and commercial livestock out. Some sections of the fence are open to allow other animals to pass in and out of the park.

further toward protecting wild animals and wild places than anything he would have accomplished as a scientist.

By the time Theodore Roosevelt left the White House, he had
accomplished more toward preserving America's wilderness than
anyone had before. While national parks already existed before
his presidency, he established a set of rules for behavior in the
parks and organized and hired rangers with the skills and authority to enforce those rules. During his time in office, Roosevelt
established 150 national forests, 51 federal bird reservations, 4

SCALE THE DEVIL

On the grasslands of eastern Wyoming, not far from the Badlands
where Theodore Roosevelt operated his cattle ranches, a single
rock tower rises 1,200 feet (366 meters) above the surrounding
plains. This featureless rock was once considered a sacred place
by the Plains Indians, who called it Bear Lodge. Today, it is known
as Devils Tower National Monument.

Devils Tower was the first national monument declared by Theodore Roosevelt after the Antiquities Act was passed in 1906. Roosevelt understood that it had special meaning for both the ranchers
and the Plains Indians. He also declared more than 1,300 acres (526
hectares) surrounding the tower as part of the monument, forever
protecting the tower and the surrounding area from development.

Today, Devils Tower is a favorite destination for rock climbers
who wish to test their climbing skills by scaling the sheer cliff while
avoiding the wide vertical cracks in the face of the rock. Climbing Devils Tower is one of the most difficult climbs in the western
United States, and climbing it requires special knowledge and skill.
Successful climbers are treated to unparalleled views of the sur-

national game preserves, and 18 national monuments. More than 230 million acres (93,077,697 hectares) of America's wilderness is protected thanks to Roosevelt's efforts.

It was not always easy for Roosevelt to convince his fellow politicians to back his conservation initiatives. America was still a relatively young nation during his presidency, and the industrial revolution had made the United States wealthy. American businessmen quickly became wealthy from exploiting the bountiful resources in the country. Timber and mineral deposits, for example, could be

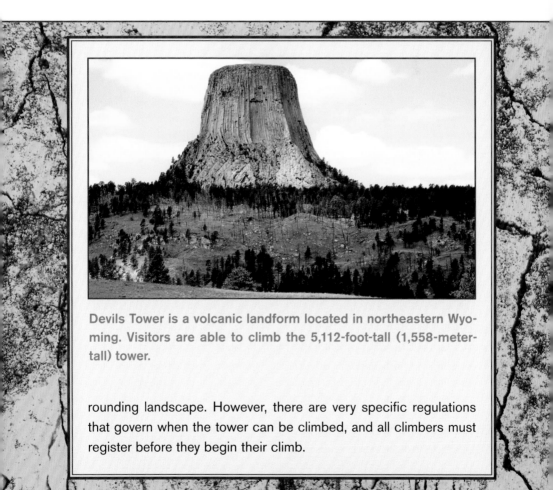

Devils Tower is a volcanic landform located in northeastern Wyoming. Visitors are able to climb the 5,112-foot-tall (1,558-meter-tall) tower.

rounding landscape. However, there are very specific regulations that govern when the tower can be climbed, and all climbers must register before they begin their climb.

excavated and sold for enormous profit. Americans believed that the resources of this country were disposable, especially the Republicans in Roosevelt's party.

In addition, when Roosevelt was president, powerful industrialists exerted great political influence and it was very difficult for Roosevelt to convince them that it was worth losing money to preserve wild places. This attitude often upset the powerful businessmen who Roosevelt needed to support him and forced him to play political games, which sometimes caused him to make unpopular decisions.

Today, more than ever, Americans understand the need to preserve natural resources. However, during Roosevelt's time, very little thought was given to their preservation. The vast prairies and huge stands of timber seemed endless and it seemed that there would be no end to natural resources. Yet Roosevelt and others knew that the day would come when Americans would use up the available resources if they were not preserved. In this way, Roosevelt was a man of vision with a keen sense of the needs of the country. Over time, his beliefs and attitudes caught on with the American public.

Since Roosevelt's time, the American public has gained an appreciation for his conservation efforts. Despite being raised in a wealthy family, Roosevelt sought to preserve America's wilderness for everyone, regardless of race or class, providing all citizens with the opportunity to enjoy America's natural resources. Other presidents have followed in Roosevelt's footsteps, including George W. Bush, who, in 2006, established the Papahanaumokuakea Marine National Monument, a collection of volcanic cliffs that is located off the northwest coast of Hawaii, covering almost 140,000 square miles (362,598 sq km).

The Boone and Crockett Club, which Roosevelt founded with George Bird Grinnell, remains in existence today and continues working to preserve America's wildlife resources. The Boone and Crockett Club works to preserve animal species, promote wise management practices, conserve habitat, and educate the public about issues involving hunting and conservation. It is still comprised of hunters just as it was when Roosevelt started the club in the 1890s. Roosevelt believed that all hunters have a responsibility to protect wild game and the habitat it lives in. Groups like the Theodore Roosevelt Conservation Partnership and Boone and Crockett carry on these traditions.

WAYS TO CONSERVE OCEAN SPECIES

The Ocean is at risk from irresponsible behavior by humans. Here are just two of the major threats that the ocean faces and ways to prevent further damage:

- **Waste**: Humans dump a tremendous amount of trash into the oceans each year. Careless boaters drop old fishing nets, soda cans, and other trash overboard instead of taking the materials back to land. These items pose a significant risk to marine species including turtles, fish, otters, dolphins, and whales. To prevent trash from getting into the ocean, place trash bags near docking areas and pick up trash along the coastline.
- **Overfishing**: Many marine species do not reproduce rapidly enough to keep up with the demand for them. Tuna, swordfish, and other predatory fish have been harvested nearly to extinction. Fishing lines and nets often kill species that are not meant to be caught. To help prevent this, contact your local congressional representative and ask them to support any bills that offer protection for marine ecosystems.

Boone and Crockett Club member, John Poston (*left*), watches George Bettas take measurements on a recently-arrived sheep mount in Bettas's office in Missoula, Montana in February 2005. The club has built a reputation as a leader in conservation efforts to help wildlife preserve habitat.

Theodore Roosevelt was a moral and virtuous man who led with a passion that few others have matched. Unlike politicians who were afraid to cross party lines or upset the status quo, Roosevelt earned his title as a maverick. He was a Republican, yet he fought against the big corporations that supported his own party. As a colonel in the army, he was a war hero who fought valiantly while many of his men were dying around him, and yet he was awarded the Nobel Peace Prize for his work to stop a war between Russia and Japan. Roosevelt was a hunter and an ardent conservationist. He left behind a landscape that might have vanished were it not for his efforts to save America's wild places. For that, we all owe Theodore Roosevelt a debt of gratitude.

How to Get Involved

These organizations provide resources to gain information and get involved in conservation issues.

The Boone and Crockett Club

http://www.boone-crockett.org

Theodore Roosevelt's conservation organization still commits time and resources to preserving America's wild places. Among their activities, the club educates hunters and hikers about responsible behavior in the woods.

Ducks Unlimited

http://www.ducks.org

Another hunter-driven conservation program, Ducks Unlimited works to protect waterfowl by preserving habitat and conducting surveys. This organization offers many outdoor programs that involve building duck boxes, helping clean up wetlands, and monitoring duck populations.

Safari Club International

http://www.safariclubfoundation.org

Safari Club International (SCI) helps conserve wild game around the world. SCI has opened the American Wilderness Leadership School in Wyoming, a camp that invites teachers and students to spend time learning about the wilderness.

Theodore Roosevelt Conservation Partnership

http://www.trcp.org

The partnership (TRCP), as it is more commonly known, encourages land owners to allow public hunting and fishing. Joining TRCP provides members with an opportunity to spread the word to landowners about conservation.

World Wildlife Fund

http://www.worldwildlife.org

The World Wildlife Fund is the world's leading conservation organization. It works in over 100 countries around the world to preserve wildlife and its habitat, providing innovative solutions to environmental challenges on both a local and global level.

Chronology

1858	Theodore Roosevelt is born in New York, New York.
1876	Roosevelt leaves home for Harvard University, in Cambridge, Massachusetts.
1878	Theodore Roosevelt's father, Theodore Senior, dies of stomach cancer.
1880	Roosevelt marries Alice Lee Hathaway.
1881	Roosevelt is elected New York assemblyman.
1882	Roosevelt publishes his book *The Naval War of 1812*.
1883	Roosevelt is reelected to a second term on New York State Assembly.
1884	Roosevelt's first daughter, Alice, is born; his wife Alice and his mother die on the same day; Roosevelt leaves New York to become a rancher in Dakota Territory.
1886	Roosevelt marries Edith Carow.
1887	Roosevelt's first son, Theodore Jr., is born.
1889	Roosevelt's second son, Kermit, is born.
1891	Roosevelt begins work as U.S. civil service commissioner; second daughter, Ethel, is born.
1894	Roosevelt's third son, Archibald, is born; his brother Elliott Roosevelt dies.
1895	Roosevelt leaves the civil service; begins working as police commissioner for the City of New York.
1897	Roosevelt is appointed assistant secretary of the Navy; his fourth son, Quentin, is born.
1898	Roosevelt leads 1st U.S. Volunteer Cavalry to success over Spanish in Cuba; elected governor of New York State.

1900	Roosevelt is elected vice president of the United States.
1901	President McKinley is assassinated; Roosevelt becomes youngest president of the United States.
1902	Roosevelt settles coal strike and dismantles Northern Securities.
1903	Roosevelt proclaims Pelican Island, Florida, a national bird refuge and begins groundwork for the Panama Canal.
1904	Roosevelt is reelected president after defeating Alton Parker.
1905	The National Forest Service is established.
1906	Passage of the Antiquities Act gives the president sole authority to proclaim national monuments; Roosevelt is awarded the Nobel Peace Prize.
1908	Roosevelt's last year in office he declines to run for president again, as promised.
1909–1910	Roosevelt goes on safari in East Africa.
1912	Roosevelt runs against President Taft as part of "Bull Moose" Progressive Party and loses to Democrat Woodrow Wilson.
1913–1914	Roosevelt travels along the River of Doubt in South America.
1918	Quentin Roosevelt killed while flying a fighter plane in World War I.
1919	Theodore Roosevelt dies at home on Sagamore Hill, in Oyster Bay, New York.

Glossary

Antiquities Act   A 1906 law that allows the president to declare national monuments without consulting the U.S. Congress

binomial nomenclature   The scientific system of naming and classifying organisms; also known as scientific name, binomial nomenclature lists the genus and species of an animal. Binomial nomenclature is always in Latin and is italicized, with the first letter of the genus capitalized.

botany   The study of plants

deforestation   The removal of forests, usually for profit

ecosystem   All of the living and non-living materials in one specific area

endangered species   Any species of animal that faces the immediate risk of extinction

evolution   Physical changes in a species over time in response to the environment

extinction   The loss of an entire species

habitat   The environment where an organism lives

invasive species   A nonnative species that is introduced and competes with native species

national forest   A forest area owned by the United States government that can be utilized by the people under the direction of the United States Forest Service

national park   An area owned by the government and managed by the National Park Service

national monument   An area that is similar to a national park but can be declared immediately when the president deems it necessary

natural resources   Objects that occur naturally in an environment that are of some use to humans, oftentimes commercial

natural selection   The idea that the organism best suited to the environment will survive and raise more offspring to adulthood

overgrazing   Too many herbivores feeding in one area, which can result in significant damage or alteration of the ecosystem

population   The number of a given species in one area at one time

species   The most specific classification of organisms

wildlife   Any organism that lives in the wild and is not domesticated by man

Bibliography

Kraft, Betsy Harvey. *Theodore Roosevelt: Champion of the American Spirit.* New York: Clarion Books, 2003.

McCullough, David. *Mornings on Horseback: The Story of an Extraordinary Family, a Vanished Way of Life and the Unique Child Who Became Theodore Roosevelt.* New York: Simon and Schuster, 1982.

Miller, Nathan. *Theodore Roosevelt: A Life.* New York: Quill, 1992.

Morris, Edmund. *The Rise of Theodore Roosevelt.* New York: Modern Library Paperbacks, 2001.

Roosevelt, Theodore. *The Autobiography of Theodore Roosevelt.* New York: Seven Treasures Publications, 2009.

Underwood, Lamar, ed. *Theodore Roosevelt On Hunting.* Connecticut: The Lyons Press, 2003.

VIDEO

American Experience: TR: The Story of Theodore Roosevelt. PBS Home Video. 1996.

Ken Burns: The National Parks—America's Best Idea. PBS Home Video. 2009.

Further Resources

Brinkley, Douglas G. *The Wilderness Warrior: Theodore Roosevelt and the Crusade for America*. New York: Harper, 2009.

Dalton, Kathleen. *Theodore Roosevelt: A Strenuous Life*. New York: Vintage, 2004.

Millard, Candice. *The River of Doubt: Theodore Roosevelt's Darkest Journey*. New York: Anchor, 2006.

Morris, Edmund. *Theodore Rex*. New York: Modern Library, 2002.

Morris, Sylvia Jukes. *Edith Kermit Roosevelt: Portrait of a First Lady*. New York: Modern Library, 2001.

Repanshek, Kurt. *Frommer's National Parks With Kids*. New York: Wiley Publishing, Inc., 2008.

Strock, James M. *Theodore Roosevelt on Leadership: Executive Lessons from the Bully Pulpit*. New York: Three Rivers Press, 2003.

WEB SITES

Cheetah Conservation Fund
http://www.cheetah.org
CCF works to preserve cheetahs by educating the public on the importance of preserving the world's fastest cat.

Sagamore Hill National Historic Site
http://www.nps.gov/sahi/index.htm
Roosevelt's beloved Sagamore Hill is listed as a National Historic Site. Today it is possible to view the President's home and the surrounding estate.

Theodore Roosevelt as President

http://www.whitehouse.gov/about/presidents/theodoreroosevelt
Roosevelt left an indelible mark on Washington politics and on the role of president. Learn more about his time in the White House through the government official site.

Theodore Roosevelt Association

http://www.theodoreroosevelt.org
Use the Research Resource link to find out how Roosevelt's ideas and policies have shaped modern America.

Theodore Roosevelt as a Conservationist

http://www.nps.gov/thro/historyculture/theodore-roosevelt-and-
conservation.htm
Visit this site to view the impact Roosevelt had on the landscape of the United States.

Picture Credits

Index

Page numbers in *italics* indicate photos or illustrations

136

About the Author

BRAD FITZPATRICK earned his bachelor's degree in biological science from Northern Kentucky University in Highland Heights, Kentucky. He has written for more than a dozen outdoor magazines including *Sports Afield*, *Midwest Outdoors,* and *African Hunter*. Brad is a member of Safari Club International, a 4-H Shooting Sports instructor, and a hunter's education instructor. He currently teaches anatomy and forensics at Southern Hills Career Center in Georgetown, Ohio.